MW00744253

Irvine Sullivan Ingram Library
DISCARD

VALUES, OBJECTIVITY, AND THE SOCIAL SCIENCES

Edited by
GRESHAM RILEY
New College

ADDISON-WESLEY PUBLISHING COMPANY

Reading, Massachusetts
Menlo Park, California
London · Don Mills, Ontario

LIBRARY
WEST GEORGIA COLLEGE
CARROLLTON, GEORGIA

This book is in the
Addison-Wesley Series in
Dialogues in the Social Sciences

Consulting Editor
Marcello Truzzi

Copyright © 1974 by Addison-Wesley Publishing Company, Inc. Philippines
copyright 1974 by Addison-Wesley Publishing Company, Inc.

All rights reserved. No part of this publication may be reproduced, stored in
a retrieval system, or transmitted, in any form or by any means, electronic,
mechanical, photocopying, recording, or otherwise, without the prior written
permission of the publisher. Printed in the United States of America. Published simultaneously in Canada. Library of Congress Catalog Card
No. 72-11888.

ISBN 0-201-06314-X
ABCDEFGHIJ-DO-79876543

Contents

Introduction

Is a value-free social science possible? If so, is it desirable? If a value-free social science is not possible, at what points and in what manner do values enter into social scientific research? And finally, if a value-free social science is a myth, is an objective social science also a myth? Questions such as these are once again in the forefront of discussions among both social scientists and philosophers of social science. In fact, not since the famous *Werturteilsstreit* (as the Value Dispute was called at the time) during the first decades of this century between Max Weber, Gustav Schmoller, and their followers has there been comparable interest in questions about values and objectivity.[1]

In part, present interest in the above questions stems from the fact that philosophers and social scientists recognize that important, practical implications follow for both the status and the role of the social sciences, depending on how these questions are answered. By the "status" of the social sciences is meant the extent to which and the sense in which they can be thought of as *scientific*. By the "role" of the social sciences is meant the extent to which they can provide knowledge that can be applied to the solution of political and social problems. Rarely do questions essentially philosophical in nature have such direct practical import.

Obviously, the limited scope of an introduction will not permit a full discussion of what it means for a discipline to be scien-

1

tific or of what the necessary and sufficient conditions are for a discipline's generating socially useful knowledge. Nevertheless, it is possible to illustrate the way in which the questions raised in the opening paragraph bear on these issues.

As Stephen Toulmin has persuasively argued in *Foresight and Understanding*, the primary aim of science is to yield not predictions or forecasts, but rather understanding.[2] If Toulmin's conclusion is accepted, the question arises: What is the nature of scientific understanding? Although "understanding" has many uses in both technical and informal discourse, one use has been dominant in the history of science. To understand something—an object, a person, a process, or an institution—is to know certain facts about it. Such knowledge has traditionally been characterized as propositional knowledge, or simply knowledge that something is the case. The facts in question may be singular, referring to specific times and places, as with demographic data; or they may be general, referring to relations among variables, as illustrated by Gresham's law in economics. In the sense in which it is used here, scientific understanding would be the goal of both ideographic and nomothetic sciences.[3]

The history of the social sciences in the twentieth century has been marked by the belief on the part of social scientists that it is indeed possible to understand (in the above sense) society, its processes, and its institutions. In particular, it has been thought that propositional knowledge can be obtained about such matters as kinship systems, socialization processes, decision-making procedures in formal governmental bodies, the intentions of heads of state, and the conditions that contribute to and reduce unemployment. On the basis of this belief it has been claimed that the social sciences qualify as scientific disciplines. Furthermore, because of the belief that propositional knowledge about societies is possible, the additional belief has existed that the social sciences can supply reliable information for the solution of social and political problems. For example, if economists possess a body of true propositions about the variables that affect unemployment, such information can be used to combat unemployment.

Many philosophers and social scientists have argued that if the social sciences are to be scientific in the sense above and if they are to be socially useful, the questions with which we opened must be answered in favor of an objective social science and in favor, if not of a value-free social science, at least of one in which the role of values does not preclude objectivity. Their reason for so arguing is the conviction that, in gaining propositional knowledge about society, social scientists are not *creating* or *constructing* a social world whose structures, relationships, and processes are dependent for their existence on the researchers' values, beliefs, wishes, sympathies, or prejudices. Rather, they are *discovering* "what is the case" with respect to the social world, discovering facts whose existence is independent of the researchers' states of mind. It is for this reason that the knowledge generated by the social sciences has been thought to be applicable to social and political problems, facets of the social world (it should be noted) that also possess an independent existence. Objectivity and value neutrality, for these philosophers and social scientists, just *is* the discovery of such facts.

For those who answer the opening questions negatively with respect to an objective, value-neutral social science, the analysis above is too simplistic. The objection is made that to draw a sharp distinction between "discovery" and "construction" fails to take account of the extensive evidence (drawn from both common experience and formal psychological studies) to the effect that a man's states of mind determine what he "sees."[4] Consequently, to think in terms of "facts" and "what is the case," as though these exist independently of man's beliefs, wishes, and values, is highly suspect. Since such thinking is suspect, the kind of understanding (propositional knowledge) to which it is said to lead is also suspect, as are the proposed "solutions" to political and social problems based on such knowledge. In fact, what counts as a problem as well as a solution to a problem is no less dependent on man's values and beliefs. Furthermore, in accord with the "relativistic" theory of knowledge that appears to be presupposed by the foregoing line of argument, one finds among critics of an objective social science the emergence of social and political *action*, as opposed to the quest for scientific *understanding*, as the proper goal of the social sciences.[5] Echoing out of the past is Marx's frequently quoted critique: "philosophers [substitute 'social scientists' for proper effect] have only interpreted the world in different ways, the point is to change it."[6] It is within this context that critics of objectivity and value neutrality are simultaneously calling into question the traditional goal of social scientific disciplines.

The practical significance of the opening questions ought to be obvious now. Should the disciplines constituting the social sciences strive to be *scientific* in the sense of increasing understanding through the discovery of propositional knowledge? Or should these disciplines serve as a base for social and political *action* that will transform the dominant institutions of society? Can social and political problems be approached with the confidence that they can be *solved* on the basis of evidence, proof, and rational argumentation? Or is it instead true that, because of the "subjectivity" of knowledge claims, these problems can only be *terminated* by nonrational techniques of persuasion or the exercise of political and other forms of power? How one answers these questions depends in part on how one answers the questions about objectivity and value neutrality in social sciences. It is for this reason that the latter questions have generated so much interest among both philosophers and social scientists.

Earlier, reference was made to the now classic *Werturteilsstreit* between Weber, Schmoller, and their followers. It will be useful in setting the stage for the essays that follow to focus briefly on two similarities between that controversy and the one that is presently taking place. First, like the dispute in Germany at the turn of the century, the present one among academicians in the United States has brought deep-seated emotions into the open. As might have been expected, strong positions pro and con have been taken. Somewhat unexpected, however, has been the division of scholars into warring camps. Indeed, discussions have transcended the bounds of a quiet, academic debate. Age and experience versus youth; conservative versus liberal; liberal versus revolutionary; establishment social science versus social science quickened by a political and social conscience—these are typical categories that have been employed to characterize the opposing forces.

To illustrate the divisiveness in question, there are, on the one flank, those who charge that the social sciences' traditional claim to value neutrality and objectivity is sheer nonsense. Such a claim, they argue, is nonsense both in *fact* and in *theory*. In *fact*, because only a casual acquaintance with the academic social sciences is required in order to be aware of their increasingly close alliance with (to use Alvin W. Gouldner's phrase) "the American

Welfare-Warfare State." Project Camelot is the *cause célèbre* that best illustrates this alliance.[7] The claim is nonsense in *theory*, the argument goes, because, as the sociology of knowledge has "shown," all knowledge claims presuppose historically relative values, interests, and classification schemes. Once the claim to value neutrality and objectivity is recognized as nonsense, however, the way is open for the emergence of a social science that is self-consciously *political*. Increasingly, this line of attack has been taken by young social scientists, using the radical caucuses of professional associations as their forum. In this volume Marvin Surkin's essay, "Sense and Non-Sense in Politics," represents this point of view.

On the other flank, as we have already suggested, are those who charge that rejecting objectivity and detached, dispassionate inquiry is equivalent to rejecting the quest for scientific understanding of society and its institutions. If all knowledge claims are ideological, what follows is that common canons of truth and validity are lost, the basis for rational discussion of social problems is eliminated, and every man becomes his own social scientist. The substitution of social-science-as-action for social-science-as-quest-for-knowledge amounts to the exaltation of obscurantism. For this reason among others, we find Robert Nisbet, in the lead essay of this volume, asserting that, next to recent attempts by radical faculty and students to destroy the university, the "most unbelievable thing at the present time" is the attack on objectivity in the social sciences.

A second similarity between the *Werturteilsstreit* and the present controversy is that each has its roots in both practical concerns and theoretical issues. As to practical concerns, the relationship between the academic social sciences and governmental agencies and the conflict over social-science-as-quest-for-knowledge versus social-science-as-action have already received comment. Important theoretical issues, only alluded to so far, are also involved. Paramount among them is a contest between competing theories of knowledge. In fact, it is this contest that gives to the controversy over values and objectivity much of its philosophical interest.

At the risk of oversimplifying a complex story, it can be stated that the competition in question is one between "empiricist" and "idealist" theories of knowledge. Although terms as vague as

"empiricist" and "idealist" have to be handled with care, they are
not without value in the present context. There is, after all, a
well-known tradition of empiricism in Western thought stemming
in modern times from David Hume and John Stuart Mill, added
to by such pragmatists as Charles Peirce and John Dewey, and cul-
minating in our century in the writings of the logical positivists.
For the greater part of the twentieth century, both physical and
social scientific thought have drawn their major epistemological
assumptions from this tradition. Among these assumptions, the
central ones are: (1) that man, in his perceptual experiences, encounters a world that exists independently of his wishes and beliefs—that is, a world whose reality is not dependent on man's
cognitive, volitional, or emotional states of mind; (2) that by
means of perception and the judgments supported by perception,
it is possible to gain knowledge of this independently existing
world; and (3) that observation and the canons of logic provide
a check on (yield confirming and infirming evidence for) hypotheses and theories rather than that hypotheses and theories determine what is perceived and dictate principles of truth and validity.
So powerful has been the influence of these assumptions that they
have contributed to the definition of what Israel Scheffler has
called the *standard view* of science, a view "shared by reflective
scientists, technical philosophers, and the educated public alike."[8]
    Although dominant, the empiricist tradition just sketched has
not had the field to itself. There is, in addition, an idealist tradition that has its foundation in the writings of Kant and Hegel, un-
derwent modifications at the hands of Marx and Mannheim, and
can be found today in the works of such diverse scholars as Ludwig
Wittgenstein, Michael Polanyi, and Thomas Kuhn. In contrast to
the major themes of empiricism, those of the idealist tradition are:
(1) the belief that perception, rather than being conceptually neutral, is structured by both linguistic categories and the mental attitudes and interests of observers; (2) the claim that the categories
in terms of which experience is organized and, in turn, known, as
well as canons of truth and validity, reflect the values and interests
of different groups at different times in history; and (3) the contention that man does not encounter reality as an uninterpreted
given but rather as something mediated or constructed by conceptual schema (Kant), ideologies (Marx), language games (Wittgen-

stein), or paradigms (Kuhn). These themes, though secondary with respect to shaping twentieth-century views on scientific knowledge, have nevertheless had their powerful spokesmen. Nowhere is this more evident than in the present debate over values and objectivity in the social sciences.

The differences between the two epistemological traditions are striking. The one assumes a world to be discovered; the other, a world that man as knower has a hand in constructing. The one assumes acts of perception that are unaffected by the observer's attitudes and interests; the other, acts of perception that are inescapably colored by expectations and prior beliefs. The one assumes the existence of data or facts that constrain belief; the other, the existence of human interests and values that determine what are to count as data or facts. And finally, the one assumes common canons of truth and validity; the other, canons that are historically relative. It is essential that these differences be kept in mind because they define the boundaries within which much of the controversy over objectivity and value neutrality is being conducted.

As to the controversy itself, the essays contained in this volume have been selected for three reasons. First, they illustrate the themes that have received attention in this introduction, namely, the emotional intensity, the practical significance, and the theoretical background of the current debate. Second, all but one are recent contributions to an old controversy. The exception is Weber's essay; all the other selections have appeared within the past decade. This is important because much of the present debate is a response to such new developments as the emergence of the radical caucuses, the increasingly close alliance between the social sciences and government, and the resurgence of interest in the sociology of knowledge and Marx's theory of ideology. And third, the essays provide an insight into the complexity of the questions with which we opened. Is an objective social science possible? That depends on what one means by objectivity. Is a value-free social science possible? That depends on what one understands by values and the manner in which they enter into social scientific research. Does a value-laden social science preclude an objective one? That depends on whether or not values are themselves subject to rational, "objective" inquiry and debate. From different perspectives the essays show why a hasty "yes" or "no" answer to these and related questions is unthinkable.

A collection of essays the size of the present one cannot cover all the issues involved in a controversy so complex as the one to which this volume is addressed. Of necessity, important aspects of the problem have been omitted. To cite only one example, the implications of Thomas Kuhn's analysis of science in terms of competing "paradigms" are far-reaching with respect to the possibilities for an objective, value-neutral social science.[9] The reader is directed to the bibliography for references to this and to other material that has not been included.

Furthermore, it would be unrealistic to think that the essays in this volume will provide conclusive answers to any of the questions raised in the opening paragraph. In fact, Max Planck's observation about the fate of new scientific ideas may be no less applicable to positions that have been taken in the debate over objectivity and values in the social sciences. Planck remarked: "A new scientific truth does not triumph by convincing its opponents and making them see the light, but rather because its opponents eventually die, and a new generation grows up that is familiar with it."[10] Although the controversy over objectivity and values in the social sciences may recur eternally, a clarification of the major issues separating the participants in the debate ought to be possible. This is the task to which the present collection of essays is directed.

NOTES

1. For a brief but informative discussion of this dispute, see Ralf Dahrendorf's "Values and Social Sciences: The Value Dispute in Perspective" in his *Essays in the Theory of Society* (Stanford, Cal.: Stanford University Press, 1968), pp. 1-18.

2. Stephen Toulmin, *Foresight and Understanding: An Enquiry Into the Aims of Science* (Bloomington: Indiana University Press, 1961).

3. For a fuller account of "scientific understanding" in the sense referred to here, see Michael Martin "Understanding and Participant Observation in Cultural and Social Anthropology," *Boston Studies in the Philosophy of Science*, edited by Robert S. Cohen and Marx W. Wartofsky, IV (Dordrecht-Holland: D. Reidel, 1969),

pp. 303-330; May Brodbeck, "Meaning and Action," *Readings in the Philosophy of the Social Sciences*, edited by May Brodbeck (New York: Macmillan, 1968), pp. 57-58; George C. Homans, *The Nature of Social Science* (New York: Harcourt, Brace and World, 1967), Ch. 1; and Ernest Nagel, *The Structure of Science* (New York: Harcourt, Brace and World, 1961). Chs. 2-3, 14-15.

4. Cf. D. C. McClelland and J. W. Atkinson, "The Projective Expression of Needs: I. The Effect of Different Intensities of the Hunger Drive on Perception," *Journal of Psychology*, 25 (1948), pp. 205-222.

5. Cf. Alan Wolfe and Marvin Surkin (eds), *An End to Political Science: The Caucus Papers* (New York: Basic Books, 1970), pp. 3-7.

6. Karl Marx, *Selected Writings in Sociology and Social Philosophy*, translated by T. B. Bottomore (New York: McGraw-Hill, 1964), p. 69.

7. See Irving Louis Horowitz, "The Life and Death of Project Camelot," *Transaction*, 3 (November/December 1965), pp. 3-7; 44-47.

8. Israel Scheffler, *Science and Subjectivity* (New York: Bobbs-Merrill, 1967), p. 7.

9. Thomas S. Kuhn, *The Structure of Scientific Revolutions* (Chicago: University of Chicago Press, 1970). Scheffler, *op. cit.*, should be consulted in this connection, for his book is a careful exploration of these implications.

10. Max Planck, *Scientific Autobiography and Other Papers*, translated by Frank Gaynor (New York: Philosophical Library, 1949), pp. 33-34.

I

Objectivity Under Attack

The first two essays, one by the sociologist Robert Nisbet and the second by Marvin Surkin, a political scientist, direct attention to the current attack on objectivity in the social sciences. Nisbet's contribution analyzes the attack; Surkin's paper levels an attack.

"Subjective, Si! Objective, No!" gives expression to Professor Nisbet's deeply felt sense of incredulity that objectivity in the social sciences should presently be repudiated, not by the public at large, but by social scientists themselves. As signs of this repudiation he cites recent declarations by radical social scientists that objectivity is not the proper goal of their disciplines and equally recent declarations by blacks and women's liberationists (among others) of the necessary ethnic and sexual roots of science. Although highly critical of young social scientists, Nisbet sees the present revolt against objectivity as stemming from developments within post-World War II academic social science, developments for which the social sciences can be justly criticized. Briefly stated, they are: (1) the hubris that led social scientists (possessing only meager research data and techniques) to seek out and to accept invitations from men of power in Washington to do consulting work on a variety of projects; (2) the affinity that has emerged since World War II between the social sciences and the military establishment; and (3) the growth of "Higher Capitalism on American campuses," which has resulted in the "New Entrepreneurs of the social sciences" merchandising their research to the highest bidder.

Marvin Surkin's "Sense and Non-Sense in Politics" is an example of what Nisbet would consider a manifestation of the present revolt against objectivity. Surkin's essay has been taken from a collection of papers written by members of the Caucus for a New Political Science, edited under the revealing title *An End to Political Science*. According to Surkin, social science's claim to objectivity and value neutrality has served only to "keep the people down" and to disguise the increasingly ideological and nonobjective role of social scientific knowledge in the service of dominant American institutions. His attack against objectivity and value neutrality is two-pronged. First, an objective, value-free social science is impossible for epistemological reasons. Since all knowledge, including methods of inquiry and techniques of data collection, is socially determined, there is an ineradicable, ideological component to all knowledge claims. Second, Surkin finds that his major thesis is supported by an empirical analysis of three frequently adopted "methodological approaches" to social science. He identifies these approaches as: (1) The New Mandarin (associated with the views of Ithiel de Sola Pool); (2) The Public Advocate (illustrated by Daniel P. Moynihan); and (3) The Persuasive Neutralist (reflected in the writings of Heinz Eulau). On the basis of this analysis, Surkin concludes that social forces inevitably decide *what* knowledge is relevant and *how* (and for what purposes) it is to be used. Consequently, the purity of social scientific knowledge, in light of its ideological function, is meaningless.

In addition to Nisbet's and Surkin's essays, the reader is directed to the following works listed fully in the bibliography: Bendix (1951); Bramson (1961), Chs. 1 and 7; Easton (1969); Gillispie (1960); Gray (1968); Scheffler (1967), Ch. 1; and Wolin (1969). The reader will also find the Winter 1970 issue of *Sociological Inquiry* valuable on this subject.

1

Subjective Si!
Objective No!

Robert Nisbet

In a memorable address to his faculty colleagues at Harvard last
Spring [1969] the economic historian Alexander Gerschenkron
likened the events there to those unfolded in the Hans Christian
Andersen tale "The Most Unbelievable Thing."

A king once offered the hand of his daughter, the princess,
to the man who could do the most unbelievable thing in the arts.
There was great competition. At last it was decided that the most
unbelievable thing among entries was a combined clock and calen-
dar of ingenious design and surpassing beauty, the product of many
years of work. Not only was the time given, the clock showed the
ages back and forth into the past and future. And circling the
clock were sculptured figures representing the greatest spiritual
and cultural minds in the history of human society.

All assembled were agreed that this clock was without question the most unbelievable thing and that the hand of the princess
must be given to the clock's handsome creator. But as judgment
was about to be pronounced, a lowbrow competitor appeared,
sledgehammer in hand. With a single blow he destroyed forever
the marvelous clock. And everybody said, why, to destroy so

Reprinted by permission from *The New York Times Book Review* (April 5,
1970), pp. 1-2; 36-37. Copyright © 1970 by The New York Times Company.

beautiful a thing, this is surely the most unbelievable thing of all. And that was how the judges had to judge.

And, Mr. Gerschenkron concluded, in our own time of troubles the most unbelievable thing, surely, is not the fragile entity that is the university, product of centuries of love of learning for its own sake, but, rather, the acts of those, whether armed with student battering ram and torch or with faculty vote, who would seek to destroy the university in a matter of days.

Most of us would agree with Mr. Gerschenkron that this is indeed the most unbelievable thing at the present time. What, then, is the *next* most unbelievable thing? The answer is possibly not so clear. There must be many entries possible. But I will suggest one: the very recently begun, fast-accumulating nihilistic repudiation in the social sciences of the ancient Western ideal of dispassionate reason, of objective inquiry, in the study of man and society.

I will come in a moment to a few of the symptoms of this ongoing repudiation of objectivity. First, though, it might be noted that as recently as 1960 had any social scientist been asked, "What is the most unbelievable thing?" he would undoubtedly have replied: "Why the fact that after many decades of effort by social scientists to achieve honored place in the community of science, we appear to be finally there." Such a social scientist could have observed that the works of such 20th-century titans as William I. Thomas, Edward Tolman, Joseph Schumpeter, A. L. Kroeber and V. O. Key—I limit myself to a few of the greater ones in this country—had at last taken effect. The august National Academy of Sciences was beginning to open its doors to social scientists as members; the physical and biological scientists on the campus had begun to make the possessive "our" include economists, sociologists, and political scientists. In a few places the hoary science requirement was being fulfilled by undergraduates with courses drawn from the social sciences. Surely, all of this would have seemed to any social scientist in 1960 as the most unbelievable thing.

But not in 1970. One is obliged by the evidence, I think, to conclude that the most unbelievable thing is the astonishing reversal of belief in the scientific, that is, the objective, the detached, the dispassionate character of the social sciences. What makes it unbelievable is that this reversal is to be found, not among physical scientists, government officials, or citizens. Not yet anyhow.

Its locus is the social sciences themselves; more precisely, in the minds of a constantly increasing number of younger social scientists and among these most crucially, of students, graduate as well as undergraduate, in the social sciences.

What are the prime manifestations of this revolt against objectivity, this scuttling of the ideal of dispassionate reason in the study of man and society? I will limit myself to two or three of the more striking ones.

First, the declaration by self-styled *radical* social scientists that objectivity of inquiry is not even a proper end of the social sciences. From radical sociologist to radical political scientist to radical anthropologist, all across the spectrum of the social sciences, the refrain is the same: "Social scientists have heretofore sought to understand society. The point, however, is to destroy and then remake society." It is not, obviously, the mature Marx, who was capable of devoting himself for many years in the British Museum to the study of capitalism and society, but the youthful romantic Marx that these voices choose to echo. If anyone thinks I exaggerate the impact at the present time of the self-styled radical social scientist, I invite him to any annual meeting of one of the learned societies.

Let us look briefly at symptom number two. It is for me somewhat more chilling inasmuch as it makes inevitable a recollection of the Nazi Rosenberg and his efforts in the 1930's to demonstrate differences between German or Aryan science on the one hand and Jewish or plutocratic science on the other. I refer here to widening belief at the present time to what can only be called the *necessary ethnic roots of science.*

It is being said, by white and black alike, chiefly with respect though to studies of blacks, chicanos, and other ethnic minorities, that it is not possible by any stretch of one's dedication to objectivity for the white to understand the black or the black to understand the white. There is black science and there is white science, and the twain shall never meet. More recently (and I can scarcely believe my eyes as I write the words) there have been intimations of a women's social science. As though one were dealing with public rest rooms.

How the gods must be laughing. We had no sooner started to erase (admittedly, *just* started) some of the more preposterous kinds of ethnic segregation in American society when there began—

and began, let it be emphasized, among those forming the vanguard of reform—to be manifest a far more deadly type of segregation: deadly because it deals with the epistemological roots of the scientific study of man.

Let us concede immediately: One must be a Negro to understand what it is like being a Negro. The same is exactly true of being a Wasp, a Puerto Rican, a mountain climber, a college professor. It is impossible for men to understand women, and women men. All of this has been said a long time, and in the sense that is usually meant I am willing to stipulate that it will always be true; just as I am willing to trumpet the imperishable truth that no one—not my wife, children, lawyer, physician, least of all, friends—will ever understand me. No one to my knowledge has ever challenged the existence in each of us, in each ethnic or cultural strain, of some doubtless forever unreachable essence. And, as the immortal Charlie Brown has concluded, it is probably good, all things considered, that this essence is unreachable.

But we are talking about science, not the metaphysics of identity or being. The movement I refer to among younger social scientists today is directed to the nature of science, *social science.* What used to be said by engineers, chemists, and the lay public is now being said by an ever widening group of social scientists themselves: particularly the younger ones. An objective understanding of social behavior is impossible; such understanding will always be limited by the political, or ethnic, or social and economic position one occupies in the social order. Its embedded values must become the values of the investigator and, hence, the bias of his conclusions. There is nothing that can be done about this.

Therefore, it behooves us to abandon the vain pursuit of knowledge, objective knowledge and to throw ourselves into action oriented toward values we can cherish. The remarkable study of conditions of classroom achievement in the schools completed a year or two ago by James Coleman, sociologist at Johns Hopkins University, cannot be believed because, first, Coleman is white and, second, his massive study was financed by the Federal Government. So runs the argument of what I can only think of as the most unbelievable thing today in the social sciences.

That it is hard to achieve objectivity, especially in the social sciences, admits of no doubt. The philosophical literature of the West is filled with notations of the idols of the mind—as they were called by Francis Bacon—that incessantly seek to engage our attention. I assume that not the most dedicated practitioner of science, even physical science, would cavil at this. In all scientific work, however good, there is no doubt some lingering element of personal predilection, some thrust that is rooted in bias.

But this said, is there, then, no significant difference between the gathering of ethnic data by an Otto Klineberg or a James Coleman, and the interpretation of these data, and the gathering and the interpretation of such data by a George Wallace? I assume all but the most hopelessly fanatical would say, yes, there is a difference. But, given the crisis of the times, the roles into which we are being forced by history and by the impending revolution, the difference is not worth emphasizing. Better, it is said, for the Klinebergs and the Colemans to abandon the idle conceit of a value-free science and to join directly the fight against George Wallace. It is quicker that way.

That it is also suicidal, on the evidence of history, seems not to enter the minds of the radical social scientists. Or if it does, it seems not to matter greatly. Without wanting to put too fine a point on the matter it is hard to resist the conclusion sometimes that this generation of the left has a rendezvous with suicide. Retreat to drugs, to sensitivity sessions, to illusory communitarianism, and to the calculatedly clownish behavior of the Chicago Seven would suggest it.

All that is beside the point. I am writing here about the revolt against objectivity I find everywhere in the country today, even among young social scientists who are not conspicuously left or conspicuously anything. There is nothing remarkable in preoccupation with objectivity. That is old. What is new is the profound difference one finds today in attitude toward the *ideal* of objectivity, toward the goal of protection from the ideals of the mind in one's work. *This* is the most unbelievable thing. . . .

What the disciples of social-science-as-action can never seem to understand is that if action is the magic word, there are always others, less burdened by the trained incapacities of scholarship, who can act more swiftly. And ruthlessly. What the man of action looks to the scholar and scientist for is knowledge, not barricade gymnastics. There is something about the cap-touching of graduate students and the genuflections of administrators' wives that unfits American university professors for the simple egalitarian civilities of the revolution.

All this would seem obvious enough; at least over Sunday morning coffee, if not Saturday night martinis. What we must ask, however, is , how is the revolution of nihilism in the social sciences at the present time to be explained? By the political objectives of the New Left, it has become fashionable to declare in academic circles—tenure circles—and by the stubborn unwillingness of members of the left to learn to become social scientists the way we did. Both explanations are variations on Original Sin. Let us look further into the matter, borrowing from the poet George Meredith: no villain need be; passions spin the plot; the wrong is mixed. Could we, the social scientists, have somehow betrayed ourselves during the past couple of decades by what is false within? Has there been anything resembling what Julien Benda called a *trahison des clercs*? I call to witness:

First, the special kind of hubris that attacked the social sciences in this country during the 1950's. With only the slenderest resources, they not only accepted invitations from all the men of power in Washington and elsewhere but actually started knocking on doors demanding invitations. Project Camelot, which can best be thought of as the social sciences' Black Sox scandal, was no doubt a fitting dénouement. (A more or less clandestine "research" project based in Washington through which more or less clandestine investigation would be made in selected foreign countries of types of insurgency and counter-insurgency. Sponsored, and heavily financed by the U. S. Army, it was mercifully killed by Executive Order before it was more than barely launched.) But even after its odor spread internationally, few American social scientists got the point. The air filled quickly with imprecations of Congress, of the Executive Office, of the State Department, and other agencies in Washington for having saved the social sciences from even worse consequences of their appalling combination of naiveté and rapacity.

Second, the vastly greater affinity that built up throughout the 1950's and 1960's between the sciences generally (but not excluding the social sciences) and the military establishment. It is, especially for the social sciences, a strange affinity. Not strange economically. That's where the money is. But Willie Sutton's celebrated words fit the robbing of banks better than they do the image of the social sciences that continued to persist in the minds of the young. Even at this very moment it is necessary to go to Congress to find substantial opposition to the affinity between the Pentagon and the sciences, social included. The latter seem to find instant absolution by repeating a hundred times a day the words "pure," "basic," and "theoretical." Few if any social scientists (except, that is, for those of the political far left) do anything beyond that save to join committees to appoint committees to find proper terminology for converting rape into legitimate union. (Stil, it's never clear just who is raping whom.)

Third, the whole emergence of the Higher Capitalism on the American campus during the 1950's. I'm not referring to the by-definition capitalist trustees. I have in mind the New Entrepreneurs of the sciences, social as well as physical, through which research started to become merchandised by the piece and the hour. In institute, bureau, and center instead of factory. Hours 8 to 5, by appointment only. By the early 1960's there were as many institute and center directors on the American campus as there were officers in the old Mexican Army. They were doing good, of course, but also doing well. That is, until the revolt came and annual meetings became Bastilles stormed by disillusioned *sans-culottes*.

The physical sciences have been spared very much in the way of revolt, and heaven knows, they began the Higher Capitalism. But physical scientists have had more sense throughout than to spice their lectures to students with quotations from Rousseau, Marx and Lenin. The social scientists thought they were being pious in so doing when in fact they were lighting matches before open kerosene. The combination of capitalist luxury in what the *Science* magazine reporter, D. S. Greenberg irreverently calls the Institute for the Absorption of Federal Funds and the ritual radicalism of its owners was to prove by 1965 to be too explosive for further containment.

There are other reasons that might be offered here. These, however, will suffice to make clear that the revolution of nihilism presently attacking that most precious of intellectual ideals, objectivity, has roots beyond the commonly cited invincible ignorance of the revolutionaries. The wrong is indeed mixed. Though I persist in believing that there are villains.

2

Sense
and Non-Sense
in Politics

Marvin Surkin

I take my cue for the title of this chapter from Merleau-Ponty, the French phenomenologist, who wrote in 1948 that "the political experiences of the past thirty years oblige us to evoke the background of non-sense against which every universal undertaking is silhouetted and by which it is threatened with failure." Merleau-Ponty refers to the experience of that generation of intellectuals for whom Marxism was a "mistaken hope" because it lost "confidence in its own daring when it was successful in only one country." But this criticism is equally relevant for a new generation of intellectuals in America who have witnessed the ideals of liberalism become little more than a superrational mystique for the Cold War, a counterrevolutionary reflex in the third world, and a narrow-range policy of social welfare at home. Merleau-Ponty argues that Marxism "abandoned its own proletarian methods and resumed the classical ones of history: hierarchy, obedience, myth, inequality, diplomacy, and police." Today intellectuals in America are marking the same critique with equal fervor about their own lost illusions.

Reprinted by permission from *An End to Political Science: The Caucus Papers*, edited by Alan Wolfe and Marvin Surkin, pp. 13-27. Copyright © 1970 by Basic Books, Inc., Publishers, New York. In the interests of simplification, the editor of the present volume has eliminated all footnotes of the original essay except those for indented quotations.

As we search for new ways to comprehend the social realities of American life and new modes of social thought and political action to reconstruct "the American dream," Merleau-Ponty's notion of sense and non-sense is useful in determining the historical relationship between ideologies and practice, between thought and action, between man and the world he creates. The dialectic of sense and non-sense dramatizes that recurrent fact in history whereby reason parades as unreason, where even "the highest form of reason borders on unreason." We must learn from recent history that "the experience of unreason cannot simply be forgotten"; that the most noble claims to universal truth, the most rational modes of philosophical or social inquiry, the most convincing declarations of political leaders are all contingent, and should be subject to revision and open to criticism and change. Marx and Kierkegaard, it should be recalled, shared in their revolt against Hegel's "Reason" insofar as the latter claimed to have attained through reason that universal truth in which history realizes itself, the real becomes rational, and the rational becomes real. The significance of this revolt against Hegelian rationalism is not its renunciation of reason itself, but rather the extent to which in Hegel's philosophical system reason is exalted and sanctified over and against the historical, human, and irrational in history.

Our primary task is therefore twofold: to recognize the historical linkage between the present social forces of reason and unreason, sense and nonsense; and unmask the guise by which the most prevalent modes of thought, their institutional expression, and their ideologies keep us from grasping their real social meaning.

My purpose in this essay is to show that the rigorous adherence to social science methodology adopted from the natural sciences and its claim to objectivity and value neutrality function as a guise for what is in fact becoming an increasingly ideological, nonobjective role for social science knowledge in the service of the dominant institutions in American society. And further, I will attempt to support the claim that the prevailing modes of inquiry in the social sciences in no way counter these recent developments in the uses of knowledge, but rather tend to reinforce them, that is, reinforce their "irrational" or, in this context, ideological uses. Moreover, I will examine what Noam Chomsky has called the double myth of the social sciences: the myth of political benevolence and the myth of scientific omniscience; the view, in other words, that since we have arrived at the end of ideology, knowledge and technology are free—neutral or nonideological—to serve the interests and powers of the "benevolent" American state and corporate elite both at home and abroad. . . .

In recent years, the burgeoning critique of behavioralism has put forward the claims that its proponents are guilty of "implicit and unrecognized conservative values," "fearful of popular democracy," and tend to "avoid political issues" in their research. It is argued, therefore, that the study of power as the observable exercise of power is conservative because it fails to consider the non-observable, non-decision-making process; that to assume that elites are the guardians of liberal democratic values and succeed in satisfying most demands made on the American polity is to be undemocratic; and that the increasing trend to build mathematical models based on the criteria of the physical sciences abstracts political science from political reality and renders such research pseudo-political or apolitical by reducing it to a sophisticated numerology.

To the contrary, however, in a recent countercritique, Bert Rockman has developed the view that these troubles of social science methodology are due to the shortcomings of the researcher, his failure to understand the role his ideology plays in his research, and the limitations of the present level of knowledge, but not to the methodology itself. Although this view is in many ways persuasive, it does not fully contend with the critique since it is obvious that one must judge social science on the basis of what it *knows* and what it *does,* not on the basis of what it *ought* to know or what it *ought* to do. For, to the extent that knowledge, including methods of inquiry and techniques of data collection, is socially determined, the social scientist's assertion of the purity of his methodology, "the quality of (his) operationalizations," his "resourceful utilization of technique," or the high moral virtue of his ideological biases are in themselves insufficient grounds for judging the results of empirical research. Bert Rockman's view, for example, is that "the only real issue is how well we are able to operationalize," which "is dependent upon what we define as reality." But the point is that what we define as reality is also dependent on preconceived knowledge, and that the validity or relevance of methods of inquiry and

the utilization of technique are also implicated in the social determination of knowledge. Therefore, the limitations of behavioral methodology are to be found even in Rockman's convincing
paper because while on the one hand he puts forward a view,
with which I fully agree, that "our 'science' will consist of developing interpretations of the political universe, based partly
on data and partly on ideology"; on the other, he concludes that
"the data should enable us to test for the invalidity of clearly defined propositions on their own terms." The latter point is ques-
tioned by even some positivists, who, like Moritz Schlick, assert
that there is an important distinction between verified knowledge and verifiable knowledge. The former is subject to tests
for validity or invalidity; but the latter, according to Schlick,
cannot be verified here and now. For example in order to prove
the proposition that God exists one must wait and see. This suggests that at least there are classes of knowledge for which the
data will not enable us to test for validity or invalidity merely on
the basis of clearly defined propositions taken on their own
terms. Does social knowledge not fall into this class of knowledge? Moreover, there is no reason to conclude that because we
have clearly defined propositions, they will necessarily be consistent with socially defined knowledge or socially acquired
street knowledge. The point was well made by Murray Kempton,
who recently noted:

> I think there is a change now in our view of life; we know
> more than we ever knew before, but we know it instinc-
> tively, and not from the sources of public information we
> get. What do we know, exactly? We know now that Walt
> Whitman Rostow is a fool. We know that Dean Rusk is a
> clerk. We know that Mr. Nixon is not really very much
> worse than the people who preceded him (which is a suffi-
> cient judgement on them), and so on. We know all these
> things not because anyone told us but because events have
> explained them to us. And it is this explanation that peo-
> ple are looking for.[1]

To criticize social science methodology and its criteria of
verification, operationalization, or objectivity is not to denigrate
the relevance of scientific inquiry. It is rather to analyze the social

and political nature of this methodology, and to see the extent to which knowledge is socially determined, the extent to which social forces decide *what* knowledge is relevant and *how* (and for what purposes) it is to be used. I will attempt to delineate three methodological approaches to social science with a view toward analyzing the linkage between scientific method and ideology or the ideological implications of research. These are (1) The New Mandarin; (2) The Public Advocate; (3) The Persuasive Neutralist.

The New Mandarin is best characterized by Ithiel de Sola Pool whose view it is that the social sciences should be devoted to the service of the mandarins of the future because psychology, sociology, systems analysis, and political science provide the knowledge by which "men of power are humanized and civilized." In order to keep the actions of the men of power from being "brutal, stupid, bureaucratic, they need a way of perceiving the consequences of public policy, that is, to describe the facts, is the primary contribution of the empirical social sciences to the uses of American power. As an example of this approach, Pool informs us of what we have learned in the past thirty years of intensive empirical study of contempory societies by formulating the central issues of order and reform in this way:

> In the Congo, in Vietnam, in the Dominican Republic, it is clear that order depends on somehow compelling newly mobilized strata to return to a measure of passivity and defeatism from which they have recently been aroused by the process of modernization. At least temporarily, the maintenance of order requires a lowering of newly acquired aspirations and levels of political activity.[2]

The meaning of this analysis for American policy is clearly in accord with counterrevolutionary American policies such as recent pacification programs, counterinsurgency and the like. But the social scientist denies that this sort of analysis is ideological, claiming instead that these studies conform to the scholarly, objective rigor of his discipline.

This is sheer non-sense. Take for example the following proposition by Professor Pool on "restructuring" government as an "empirical" formulation: "I rule out of consideration here a

large range of viable political settlements" for restructuring government in South Vietnam, namely, those that involve "the inclusion
of the Viet Cong in a coalition government or even the persist-
ence of the Viet Cong as a legal organization in South Vietnam."
Such arrangements "are not acceptable" since the only acceptable
settlement is one "imposed by the GVN despite the persisting
great political power of the Viet Cong." While it may be argued,
as Pool puts it, that "the only hope for humane government in
the future is through the extensive use of the social sciences by
government," the precise ideological nature of this new role, all
claims of objectivity to the contrary, is not to be denied. In effect, intellectual detachment and the disinterested quest for
truth—the professed essence of the value-free, neutral social scientist—are replaced by the new elite role of the masters of knowledge whose knowledge is placed at the disposal of the "benevolent" political interests of the masters of power. Accordingly,
social scientists become, in essence, "house-ideologues for those
in power."

The Public Advocate appears to be a more selfless servant
of the people who is concerned primarily with reforming public
policy to better the lot of the poor, disfranchised, or underdeveloped. His professed mission is to serve the public good rather
than the government or the corporation. In response to the
plight of the poor and black in America, Daniel P. Moynihan
adopts the stance of the Public Advocate. He decries the failures of the War on Poverty to contend with the "problem." His
view is that the problem of poverty cannot be solved either by
discouraging the rigorous inquiry into the social process that
keeps men in poverty (or leads them out of it), or by falling back
on the guilt complex of the white society which concludes that
"white racism is essentially responsible for the explosive mixture
which has been accumulating in our cities since the end of World
War II." Rather, for Moynihan, "American social science can do
better, and so it ought." This requires commitment on the part
of the social scientist—the War on Poverty was such a commitment—and an honorable desire to be helpful. Therefore, even
though there were many failures in the War on Poverty program,
the commitment by social scientists and the government for
which they worked was made, and "that commitment stands,

and intellectuals, having played a major role in its establishment, now have a special responsibility both for keeping it alive and for keeping it on the proper track."

The Public Advocate uses his social science knowledge to influence public policy, but he is not, so it is claimed, the servant of government since his primary objective is "to get public policy to react to unmet social demands. . . ." However, the research design, the questions posed, and the general framework of the analysis are all circumscribed by the Public Advocate's desire to do something *for* the poor and black people insofar as that "something" is possible within the known or assumed limits of the existing institutions. For the Public Advocate, "simply to blame the system is . . . obscurantism" and best left out of consideration. He prefers to limit his research to influencing policy within the system—to make the system work better. The Public Advocate assumes, therefore, the values of the system and its operationality as given; he does not question it. Whatever the case may be, he has obviously not arrived at this analysis by empirical, objective, or neutral investigation.

In the Moynihan Report on the Negro family, "doing something for these people" was described in a special research report for the internal use of the government. The report revealed a pattern of instability in the Negro family structure which represented a "tangle of pathology . . . capable of perpetuating itself without assistance from the white world." In addition, Moynihan adduced evidence to show that illegitimacy, crime and juvenile delinquency, drop-out rates and unemployment were "causally" connected to family structure. The social scientist has here uncovered a case of deviant social pathology, the cure for which is to change the deviants, not the system. Christopher Jencks criticizes Moynihan's conservative analysis because "the guiding assumption is that social pathology is caused less by basic defects in the social system than by defects in particular individuals and groups which prevent their adjusting to the system."

The major concern of the Public Advocate is not knowledge in itself but the policy relevance of his research findings. When he writes "a polemic which makes use of social science techniques and findings to convince others," it should be clear that he expects that "the social science data he could bring to bear would have a persuasive effect." Therefore, the scholarly or "scientific" quality of his research or its political relevance for those whom he wants to help would seem to be of only secondary importance. The Public Advocate is committed primarily to advocating ways by which the existing social institutions can be made to function better. However broad a range of research or policy this may include, it is nonetheless limited to the established parameters of the system, and thus it appears that the Public Advocate always tends to tell the government what it wants to hear, i.e., to constantly reinforce existing myths and ideologies or create "a new set of myths to justify the *status quo*." In no way does this qualify the Public Advocate as an objective or value-free social scientist.

The only remaining question is whether and to what extent this sort of policy science is defined by and serves the interests of governmental agencies at the expense of the public. Herein lies the background of nonsense characterized by the Public Advocate's desire to do something *for* those poor, black people while knowing that in a very real sense his commitments are elsewhere. Julius Lester has correctly perceived the social and political function of the Public Advocate when he says. "Bang! Bang! Mr. Moynihan, " because

> somehow . . . nothing is true for a white man until a white man says it. Let the black say the same thing, and it will not be heard, or, if heard, ignored. Let a white man say it, and it becomes truth. It should be obvious why it will be the Moynihans we go after first rather than the southern sheriff.[3]

On the surface, the case of the *Persuasive Neutralist* seems to be altogether different from the first two types, for while the New Mandarin and the Public Advocate are ideologues for the existing social system, the Persuasive Neutralist appears as a professional methodologist who is concerned "strictly" with the techniques and knowledge brought forth by the scientific or "behavioral" revolution in the social sciences. His studies are generally not policy-oriented, though he claims that policy studies may also be "objective," and he carefully eschews any sign of ideological intent in his research. The Persuasive Neutralist, not unlike the other types, may have a calling, but it is to science, not polemics, dogma, or ideology. His main function is to cumulate knowledge about the social world, *to describe, understand and interpret reality, not change it.*

In my view, however, the Persuasive Neutralist is equally subject to the claim of nonobjectivity, of ideology and non-sense stated above. The view, for instance, that one's research objective is to describe reality but *not* to change or criticize it is, I would argue, fundamentally conservative and will generally tend to reinforce existing institutions and social patterns. But I think the critique can be extended further than I have thus far suggested.

First, behavioral social scientists make the basic claim that the world of thought and knowledge is objective and rational. The social scientist so oriented adapts the intellectual posture of the physical scientist whose main function is to observe the phenomena of his chosen sphere of social reality and organize his data in such a way that he will be able to understand, interpret and, hopefully, explain that segment of the world under observation. His work is piecemeal; he theorizes and hypothesizes and later, by employing the techniques of modern technology and science, cumulates data, replicates experiments, and amasses evidence for his propositions. In all events, his research is the work of the rational thinker, the "scientist," but one who is constrained by the self-imposed rules of the physical sciences to see the world from the outside, as a neutral observer. Naturally, he is also constrained in his view of social reality because for him the world is what "I think," not what "I live through." This world of science is the natural or physical world which reason alone (scientific or conceptual knowledge) can harness; but it is not the world of man and society which is always composed of reason and unreason, preconceptual knowledge and conceptual knowledge, thought and action, objective and external phenomena as well as subjective and internal phenomena. In short, for the behavioral scientist, "scientific" knowledge can overcome irrationality, contingency, and subjectivity. However, by its very nature, this knowledge has definite limitations, which William James clearly perceived when he distinguished "knowledge-about" or thought knowledge from "knowledge by acquaintance" or felt knowledge. To be empirical, according to James and contemporary phenomenologists, requires the distinction and elucidation of these different levels of knowing and meaning construction if the object of inquiry in social science is the social and human world itself. For James, "feelings are the germ and starting point of cognition, thoughts the developed tree," and therefore, a genuine empiricism "cannot simply construct experience as a logical patterning tailored to the convenience of this or that analysis of what valid propositions require." Rather, "we must inquire into the ways in which logical order can relate to the concretely felt experience."

Moreover, the claim of objectivity in behavioral social science is not warranted by the facts. Since objectivity refers to only external, observable, physical phenomena—the things of the world— it fails to recognize precisely those human and social experiences which also include internal, subjective, and psychical phenomena. What is essential for social science is the recognition that:

> Human behavior is neither a science of blind reactions to external "stimuli," nor the project of acts which are motivated by the pure ideas of disembodied, wordless mind. It is neither exclusively subjective nor exclusively objective, but a dialectical interchange between man and the world which cannot be adequately expressed in traditional causal terms.[4]

To put it in other words, human behavior and human knowledge are neither exclusively rational nor exclusively irrational. The quest for exclusivity from either side simply has no scientific foundation when applied to men and society. To the contrary, behavioral science is primarily concerned with theory construction and scientific *testability* rather than social *tenability*. Models tend to be viewed as theories (provable or disprovable cause-effect propositions) which purport to forecast practical results, i.e., game theory or the domino theory. The replicability of experiments or the uniformity of data are given the status of causal explanation. In contrast, Max Weber asserted that

> ... If adequacy in respect to meaning is lacking, then no matter how high the degree of uniformity and how precisely its probability can be numerically determined, it is still an incomprehensible statistical probability whether dealing with overt or subjective processes.[5]

In order to avoid the objectivism and intellectualism of science, one must recognize this dependence of conceptualization on the preconceptual life-world, which Husserl called the *Lebenswelt*, because:

> The whole universe of science is built upon the world as directly experienced, and if we want to subject science itself to rigorous scrutiny and arrive at a precise awareness of its meaning and scope, we must begin by reawakening the basic experience of the world of which science is the second-order expression. . . . To return to things themselves is to return to that world which precedes knowledge, of which knowledge *speaks*, and in relation to which every scientific schematization is an abstract and derivative sign-language, as is geography in relation to the countryside in which we have learnt beforehand what a forest, a prairie or a river is.[6]

Insofar as behavioral scientists ignore this social "reality," insofar as they fail to distinguish scientific facts or natural reality from world facts or social reality, their research tends to objectify or reify human and social meaning. There can be no doubt that behavioral social science has amassed "knowledge-about," but the capacity for this knowledge to reconcile its theoretical understanding of social problems with the experienced reality of, say, the black power advocates, and employ it in the quest for free, creative social activity and responsive social institutions is today indeed questionable.

Second, it is becoming more evident with recent trends in the uses of technical and social science knowledge by large-scale institutions that science and technology are not necessarily progressive, as it was once thought. As John McDermott has recently noted:

> Segments of knowledge still belong to technical specialists and pieces of knowledge to the well educated, but only the very largest organizations are able to integrate these proliferating segments and pieces into systems of productive, effective, or more likely, profitable information. That is the meaning of technological progress: the systematic application of new knowledge to practical purposes. And it dictates a continual increase in the size, wealth and managerial capacity of

the organizations which seek thus to apply knowledge. Corporations, government agencies, universities and foundations have been quick to respond.[7]

In the face of this technological explosion and increasing institutionalization and professionalization of knowledge, to claim a neutral or "objective" role for social science is clearly to fall under the onus of what Merleau-Ponty called "non-sense." Briefly put, the full thrust of reason and knowledge is being turned against itself—against truth and humanity, in favor of the dominant institutions and power-centers which are now tending to the *manipulation,* rather than the *liberation* of mankind, especially its underclasses. In short, the Persuasive Neutralist who inveighs against the ideologies and utopias that want to change the world in favor of a scientific or "objective" description or interpretation of social reality turns objective knowledge upside down: a fundamentally apolitical posture becomes highly political or ideological insofar as that knowledge serves entrenched institutions and power interests, whether these be pacification programs in South Vietnam or funneling of the energies of black youth into the established channels of American society. To put it another way, the meaning and social significance of rational inquiry is inverted—sense is turned into nonsense. . . .

Finally, in terms of the ideological implications of social science, some behavioral scientists have taken the position that the recognition and clarification of their own biases will be sufficient to place such biases in perspective, enable them to then get on with the pursuit of science. This view is rightly attacked by Heinz Eulau, a well-known behavioralist. Eulau's argument is that one's science is either value-free or it is not. It "is a problem of fact," exhorts Eulau, "that can be answered only through empirical research into the nature of science as a form of human activity." The only quibble I have with Eulau, whose view is representative of most behavioral thought is the assumption about the value-free study of politics he makes. In reference to policy science, Eulau writes: "The policy science approach does not assume that a value-free scientific study of politics is impossible because men pursue values through politics. Indeed, it sharply distinguishes between propositions of fact that are believed to be subject to scientific-empirical inquiry, and propositions of value for which empirical science has as yet no answer." Accordingly, the policy scientist can avoid violating the canons of scientific method by recognizing the existence of both facts and values and keeping a subtle balance or distance between them. Therefore, Eulau concludes, this approach " does not deny that scientific research on propositions of fact cannot serve policy objectives; indeed, it asserts that political science, as all science, should be put in the service of whatever goals men pursue in politics." But the keynote of Eulau's position gives a telling commentary on all three approaches when he asserts that science is still value-free even if "there is nothing in his science that prevents its being used for ends of which he disapproves."

Despite his claims of value-neutrality, Heinz Eulau's conclusions could not be more insightful. Social science is always used by societies which generally determine what knowledge will be used and how knowledge will be used. The purity of knowledge is meaningless as long as that knowledge is used by social institutions for certain prescribed purposes. Hence, social knowledge, whether it be scientific or not, has a value for that society and plays a function which can most often be called ideological. Alas, we have come full circle back from the Persuasive Neutralist to the New Mandarin and Public Advocate. The differences could not have been very significant from the start.

American society is in need of a radical reorganization of social priorities. To achieve that end may call for a reconstruction of its dominant institutions, but at the least requires a redistribution of power and wealth as well as a redistribution of knowledge. The need for radical change grows as America's institutions find it increasingly difficult to meet the rising social demands of its most needy, most powerless, most alienated members. The vision of a white, liberal power structure bent on exploiting and repressing the poor and black at home and fighting counterrevolutionary, imperialist wars abroad is becoming more evident to the underclasses, left intellectuals, and students. What they envisage is the rationalization of bureaucracy, the monopolization of power and wealth, the tailoring of knowledge and technology, and the manipulation and control of the people in the interests of self-serving elites—managerial, corporate, political, and intellectual. To argue to the contrary is of no avail since this generation has experienced (and is becoming more conscious of) its own poverty, powerlessness, alienation, and knows how these feelings relate to the reality of American power and ideology in Vietnam and Santo Domingo, Watts and Detroit, Chicago and Columbia University. To plead for reason, detachment, objectivity or patience in the face of abject poverty, political repression, and napalmed women and children is absurd. Along with the power structure, reason, they will tell you, is what gets us into Vietnam and keeps us there, produces a war on poverty but curtails funding, calls for "law and order" instead of freedom and justice. Moreover, what I have argued in this essay is that in spite of all claims to objectivity, rational, intellectual output, whether in the form of policy programs at home or pacification programs abroad, tends to reinforce the established order. That this may occur was underscored even by Heinz Eulau. In fact, the meaning of so much rational model-building, statistical data, theorizing, planning and programming can be viewed—as it is viewed by many of those most affected—as an elaboration of new, sophisticated techniques for "keeping the people down." This is the ideological significance of so-called "objective" or "scientific" knowledge as many have come to know it or experience its results.

NOTES

1. David Gelman and Beverly Kempton, "The Trouble with Newspapers: An Interview with Murray Kempton," *The Washington Monthly*, 1 (April 1969), p. 26.

2. Cited in Noam Chomsky, *American Power and the New Mandarins* (New York: Pantheon Books, 1969), p. 36.

3. Julius Lester, *Look Out, Whitey: Black Power's Gon' Get Your Mama* (New York: Grove Press, 1968), p. 54.

4. Maurice Merleau-Ponty, "Foreword" in his *The Structure of Behavior* (Boston: Beacon Press, 1963), pp. xv-xvi.

5. Max Weber, *The Theory of Social and Economic Organization* (New York: Free Press, 1966), p. 88.

6. Maurice Merleau-Ponty, *Phenomenology of Perception* (London: Routledge and Kegan Paul, 1962), pp. viii, ix.

7. John McDermott, "Knowledge is Power," *The Nation* (April 14, 1969), p. 458.

II

Perspectives on Objectivity

In a carefully reasoned selection, "On the Objectivity of Social Science," the philosopher Richard S. Rudner contends that, because of a systematic ambiguity in the use of the term "objectivity," it is difficult to assess the charge that an objective social science is impossible. The ambiguity he pinpoints is the use of "objective" and its polar opposite, "subjective," to mean "nonpsychological" and "psychological," respectively, and a use that means "unbiased" and "biased," respectively. Of these two uses, it is the latter, Rudner argues, that is relevant to the controversies over the status of the social sciences.

Given the use of "objective" to mean "unbiased," Rudner suggests that the predication of the term to *methods of inquiry* is the most promising context within which the charge of nonobjectivity in the social sciences can be leveled. From the standpoint of methodology, he examines two formulations that the charge might receive: (1) the scientific method is itself nonobjective, and therefore its employment by the social sciences warrants the charge; and (2) although the scientific method is objective, the unique subject matter of the social sciences requires for its investigation a less objective method. Rudner argues that both formulations are indefensible.

The first formulation is indefensible because it presupposes that in order to be objective a method of inquiry must preclude the possibility of error. But as Rudner correctly observes, such an assumption misconstrues the nature of *empirical* inquiry. A method of empirical inquiry can never make error impossible; it can only minimize the likelihood of error.

Professor Rudner "unpacks" the second formulation in the following manner. The social sciences have been thought unique in that the subject matter they investigate is the *meaning* of social behavior. There are two senses, however, in which social behavior has been said to possess meaning. It possesses meaning in the sense of having "importance or value" and in the sense of being "rule-governed." Rudner associates Max Weber with the first position and Peter Winch (see *The Idea of a Social Science*) with the second. Although Weber and Winch interpret *meaningfulness* differently, they agree that the scientific method is wholly inappropriate to its investigation. Furthermore, they agree that a special method is required, one involving empathic acts, which reproduces the conditions or states of affairs being studied.

Rudner finds Weber's and Winch's arguments singularly uncompelling. Both are guilty of what he calls the "reproductive
fallacy," namely, the mistaken belief that anything one is to understand has to be reproduced for direct inspection. In opposition
to this belief, Rudner reminds the reader of Einstein's remark that
it is not the function of science to give the taste of soup. In other
words, the task of science (both physical and social) is to describe
and to explain the world, not to duplicate it. Once this principle
is grasped, Rudner argues, there is no reason to think that "social
science must fail of achieving the methodological objectivity of
the rest of science or that social science must employ a radically
distinct methodology."

The selection by the sociologist Alvin W. Gouldner is the
concluding section of his lengthy paper "The Sociologist as Partisan: Sociology and the Welfare State" (Gouldner, 1968). In this
section he distinguishes three meanings that "objectivity" might
have for the sociologist: (1) transpersonal replicability; (2) normative objectification; and (3) personal authenticity. "Transpersonal replicability" — defined as the description of one's research procedures so explicitly that others employing them on the
same problem will come to the same conclusion — is the least important of the three. It is simply an operational definition that
specifies what must be done in order for a hypothesis to be class-
ified as objective. What "objectivity" means "conceptually and
connotatively" is left unclarified. Though dismissed as the least
informative definition, "transpersonal replicability" provides a
valuable backdrop for a brief discussion of Max Weber's views on
science and morality. Professor Gouldner's observations should
be read in conjunction with the Weber essay reprinted in this volume, for they provide a useful commentary on Weber's position.

Gouldner's positive analysis of objectivity is developed
around the phrases "normative objectification" and "personal authenticity." Briefly stated, his position is that sociological research
is analogous to the rendering of a legal decision. The impartiality
or objectivity of a judge is determined, however, not on the basis
of his distributing costs and benefits equally between the parties
in conflict, but on the basis of his allocating costs and benefits in
conformity with some stated normative standard. The problem of
objectivity both in law and in sociology, Gouldner argues, is one
of working one's way through to a value commitment. For the

sociologist no less than for the judge, this means not deceiving others concerning the value basis of his professional judgments. This is what Gouldner means by objectivity in the sense of normative objectification. Closely related to the imperative not to deceive *others* is the imperative not to deceive *one's self* concerning the normative basis of one's judgments. This is what Gouldner means by objectivity in the sense of personal authenticity. If a person engages in self-deception, Gouldner contends that he reduces thereby his capacity to acknowledge hostile information — that is, "information that is discrepant with our purposes, hopes, wishes, or values." To be closed to hostile information, however, is to sacrifice objectivity altogether. For Gouldner, therefore, the pursuit of objectivity rests upon the having of values and the honest reporting of values held. Not only is an objective social science compatible with a value-laden social science; the latter is a necessary condition for the former.

Additional readings relevant to this section include: Diesing (1966); Gewirth (1954); Gibson (1960); Gillispie (1960); Heelan (1970); Martin (1971); Myrdal (1969); Nagel (1961); and Scheffler (1967).

3

On the Objectivity
of Social Science

Richard S. Rudner

A. 'Objectivity'

Closely connected with the view that some peculiarity of social
phenomena precludes using the scientific method to investigate
them, is the view that the social sciences cannot achieve "objectivity." The difficulty in assessing this charge . . . is, in part, the
obscurity that attends the charge itself. Specifically, it is frequently not at all clear what those who level the charge have in mind in
their uses of the term 'objectivity.' Before we can properly evaluate the cogency of the charge we must see if it is possible to become
clear about some of the appropriate meanings of this key term.

A pivotal source of the confusion that has attended uses of
the term 'objectivity' stems from a remarkable ambiguity which
'objective' and its polar-opposite, 'subjective,' have had inflicted
on them (in part by a traditional metaphysical view, the apparent
popularity and vitality of which is out of all proportion to the
number of times it seems to have been discredited in the history
of philosophy). The ambiguity involved stems from being unclear
about those uses of 'subjective' and 'objective' that mean something very much like 'psychological' and 'nonpsychological' res-

From Richard S. Rudner, *Philosophy of Social Science,* pp, 73-83. Copyright © 1966. Reprinted by permission of Prentice-Hall, Inc., Englewood
Cliffs, N. J.

pectively, and those uses of 'subjective' and 'objective' that mean
something like 'biased' (or 'error-laden') and 'unbiased' (or 'error-
free') respectively.

Now, these *are* quite distinct pairs of meanings, and mixing
them up in the controversies that have raged over the status of the
social sciences has been an especially fertile source of many of the
confusions that haunt the voluminous literature of these controversies. Notice, for example, that if (adopting now the metaphysical position alluded to above) we routinely were to *identify* the referent of 'subjective' in the sense in which the term applies simply
to psychological states, with the referent of that term in the sense
in which the term is roughly synonymous with 'biased,' then the
result of that identification would be that such perfectly useful
locutions as 'take an objective approach to' or 'look at from an objective point of view' or 'evaluate objectively,' and many similar locutions, would have to be regarded as gibberish. For on this assumption the locution 'unbiased viewpoint' would be self-inconsistent.

No one has ever demonstrated that the psychological, per se,
is identical with the biased; nor is it easy to imagine how a cogent
demonstration of this could possibly proceed. (The fact that metaphysical positions have *assumed* this position without demonstration is scarcely a recommendation for its adoption.) To adopt it
would tend, in fact, to obscure a problem that does appear to be
of considerable importance, namely, that concerned with *which*
psychological states or processes can justifiably be said to be instances of bias, and which cannot.

In employing the terms 'subjective' and 'objective' we will,
accordingly, be careful to make clear which of the alternative
meanings of the two terms is at issue. In the controversies over
the status of the social sciences it is clear that the questions have
centered around whether unbiased investigation of (broadly speaking) psychological phenomena is possible, rather than around the
absurd question of whether nonpsychological (the alternative meaning) states of knowledge are attainable. Thus, in coming to assess
the charges against the social sciences we shall, in fact, be concerned
with what sense it makes to speak of social science as being irreme-
diably biased.

In the relevant sense of our discussion, 'objective' has, in fact,
been used to apply to at least four different things: (1) the verisi-

militude of ideas, i.e., the replicalike character of mental imagery, (2) the truth of statements, (3) the reliability of methodologies, and (4) the psychological disposition of an investigator to have, or believe, or employ the kinds of ideas, statements, or methodologies mentioned under 1, 2, or 3. It is evident that 'unbiased' or 'objective,' in the sense of 4, is derived from the preceding three senses, and we shall, accordingly, confine our brief analyses to 1, 2, and 3 on the assumption that 4 would present no (relevant) special problems were 1, 2, and 3 to be satisfactorily clarified.

1. *'Objectivity' as a Predicate of Ideas.* The view that objectivity is to be found in a certain correspondence between our ideas—construed somewhat naively as mental imagery or picturizations—and those things of which they are ideas, has often been attributed to John Locke (however justifiably is not at issue here). Whatever may have been the precise nature of Locke's views, there can be little doubt that many people have held, and many continue to hold, that our mental picturizations in this sense are objective, insofar as they exactly resemble what they are "pictures" of. This is a sort of snapshot theory of objectivity.

However, despite the popularity of this man-in-the-street notion of objectivity, it has some formidable difficulties: (*a*) The sense of 'exact resemblance' that it involves is quite obscure. Are our mental images supposed to be as tall, heavy, dry, or smooth textured as those things of which they are mental images? If so, in what sense? If not, what is meant by 'resemblance'? It may be possible to overcome these difficulties and give satisfactory answers to such questions, but even the beginning of an attempt to do so reveals that the "snapshot" theory of objectivity is not nearly so straightforward or uncomplicated as it may initially have appeared. (*b*) It is *not* the case that all of our ideas of extraideational entities are picturizations. Not all of our mentation can by any means be construed as pictorial in character; and if this is true, what can be meant by 'resemblance' between our *nonpictorial* ideas and that of which they are ideas? The "snapshot" theory of objectivity provides us with no means for dealing with such problems. (*c*) Most crucial, perhaps, is the fatal defect in the fundamental assumption that underlies the entire position; for this view of objectivity seems to presuppose that we can in some mysterious way *directly* compare our ideas with something we would have to know 'nonideationally.' The very grammar of 'comparing' in this context entails *ob-*

serving or *perceiving* or *sensing* or *knowing*, etc., the things to be compared. But to do this for one of the pair as the position demands, without having any "mental contents"—to go *out of our minds*, so to speak, in just the sense the position appears to require—is to seek to fulfill a self-contradictory or nonsensical requirement. And the "snapshot" theory accordingly seems as obscure or self-inconsistent as is the criterion of objectivity it presupposes.

2. *'Objectivity' as Truth.* The sense of the term 'true' (or 'false') throughout this book is, in general, that of the *semantic conception of truth*, which implies that 'true' and 'false' are construed as predicates that apply to linguistic entities, i.e., sentences (or in our slightly broader usage, statements). It follows that extralinguistic entities are neither true nor false—existence may be claimed or denied for such nonlinguistic entities but not, properly, truth or falsity. It is what we *say* about extralinguistic entities, our accounts of them or descriptions of them, that are either true or false. Consequently, to identify objectivity with truth is to make 'objectivity' a predicate of statements. And indeed there does appear to be a well-entrenched usage of the term in which it is employed in just this sense. Thus, for example, when we speak of someone as giving "a factual, or objective, account" of something, we appear to be saying little more than that it is a true account.[1] This view of the nature of objectivity, unlike the preceding one, seems relatively unproblematical.

3. *'Objectivity' as a Predicate of Methods.* Predicating 'objectivity' of sentences by no means exhausts the well-entrenched uses to which the term is put; consider 'he adopted an objective mode of investigating the facts' or 'he proceeded to inquire in an objective manner' or 'he employed an objective method in investigating . . . ,' etc. Here, it seems obvious that the application of the term is not to sentences, but to means or methods of conducting inquiries. In terms of our present concern, this must be regarded as an application to the methodology, logic, or criteria of validation that we adopt in conducting inquiries. What is needed, accordingly, for this usage, is an analysis of just what is being asserted when we claim that one methodology is objective, or more objective than another.

In asserting that one method is more objective than another, we appear to be claiming that it is more *reliable* than that other.

And the sense of 'reliability' involved would appear to be satisfied by the following criterion: Method A is more reliable than Method B if, and only if, its continued employment is less liable to error (i.e., is less likely to result in our continuing to believe, or coming to believe, false sentences). Correspondingly, we might say that a method was "maximally reliable" if, among all alternatives, it minimized the likelihood of error in this sense. Again correspondingly, we might say that a method was "absolutely reliable" if it made error impossible.

This account enables us to take explicit note of some generally useful characteristics involving the attribution of objectivity to methods. It can be seen at once that the demand that a method of *empirical* inquiry (i.e., inquiry into matters of fact) be absolutely reliable (absolutely objective) is self-contradictory; this is similar to the demand that a circle be squared or that a precise terminating decimal value be given for the number π. Empirical inquiry is, *logically*, not the kind of inquiry that can be undertaken in a manner to make error impossible. Next, among the various methodologies advocated in the course of intellectual history for the investigation of the universe, none has been shown to be more reliable than the method of science. This is due in part to science's insistence on *corrigibility*—the insistence that any hypothesis, however well-confirmed, may be susceptible to *disconfirmation* in the light of future investigation. The books, so to speak, are never closed on any hypothesis in the precise sense that evidence relevant to the confirmation or disconfirmation of it can never be exhausted. Accordingly, it is fair to say that if a hypothesis we accept is false, the continued application of scientific method to its investigation will increase the likelihood that we will be able to correct our error by coming upon evidence that disconfirms it. It is in this sense, of a systematically built-in mechanism of corrigibility, that the intellectual history of the species has presented man with no more reliable (i.e., in sense 3, no more objective) method of inquiry than that of science.

B. The Objectivity of Social Science

Our survey of various relevant senses in which the terms 'objective' and 'subjective' (or 'nonobjective') have been used now places us in a better position to assess the specific charge the the social sciences fail in attaining objectivity. Patently, the charge must amount to an attribution of bias in social science if it is to be regarded as a nontrivial charge. At the same time we can dismiss the charge in the sense of 1 or 2 above as being clearly unwarranted —in the sense of 1 because, as we have seen, the sense of 'objectivity' it presupposes is itself too defective and obscure to be credited; in the sense of 2 because it comes to the claim that the social sciences are precluded from the acquisition of any true hypotheses or theories. This latter charge is obviously refuted by the fact that social scientists have in the past believed, and doubtless will continue to believe, *contradictory* hypotheses (i.e., hypotheses that contradict other hypotheses believed by social scientists). Of course we may not know, or we may not have good evidence for deciding, which of a contradictory pair of sentences is true; but it is logically necessary that one of every such pair should *be* true. Since there is no reason to believe that some social scientists will fail in the future to accept hypotheses that are the contradictories of hypotheses accepted by other social scientists (or indeed, by themselves in the past), we may reasonably conclude that social science has neither been nor will be precluded from the acquisition of some true hypotheses.

However, the charge of nonobjectivity is not likely to have been leveled in precisely the sense of 2—certainly not by any serious thinker who has been aware of its import as just outlined. In fact, we must seek the serious instances of the charge among those who have intended it in relation to 3.

From the point of view of methodology, then, the charge of nonobjectivity may be construed in either of at least two ways: (*a*) the scientific method is nonobjective and therefore its employment in the social sciences warrants the charge against them; (*b*) the social sciences must by their nature employ a less objective method of inquiry than the scientific method.

If we interpret the charge as being directed in general against the reliability of the scientific method itself, there again seem to be no decisive reasons for crediting the charge. In the light of what we have said above, the claim that the method of science is not *absolutely objective*, for example, would be seen to be defective as well as based on a misconstrual of the nature of empirical inquiry. But no alternative methodology has been shown to be more objective than—or even as objective as—the method of science. Indeed, there is good reason to believe that the method of science is maximally objective. Finally, it is clear that the charge against the scientific method in general does not place the social sciences in any more invidious a position than the nonsocial sciences; accordingly, it is difficult to take seriously any such arguments, which purport to be establishing a peculiarly nonobjective status for social science.

The alternative interpretation of the charge that social science is without methodological objectivity—and the last one we are to consider—takes a position in some ways diametrically opposed to the one just mentioned. It concedes, or at least does not question, the objectivity of the scientific method, but holds instead that the social sciences cannot use such an objective method; the social sciences must either eschew or supplement the use of the scientific method in such a fashion that the resulting methodology falls short of the degree of objectivity characteristic of the scientific method.

This argument is, in fact, close to those allegations . . . concerning the impossibility of a social science that stem from a supposed complexity or other alleged peculiarity of social phenomena. Accordingly, we can perhaps do no better than to examine Max Weber's well-known espousal of this view, a view argued at least as persuasively by him as by anyone else who has come along since he wrote on the topic.

Weber offers a variety of arguments for his position on the irremediable (methodological) subjectivity of the social sciences. . . . But two . . . closely related arguments deserve detailed consideration. These begin with premises about the character of social phenomena and the aim of social inquiry, and proceed to conclusions about the inadequacy of the scientific method to fulfill this aim, the need to supplement the scientific method by special methodological adjuncts peculiar to social science, and end with the claim that these special but indispensable adjuncts render social science methodologically nonobjective.

What (according to Weber and others) renders social phenomena idiosyncratic is the quality of *meaningfulness* that typically attaches to such phenomena. Moreover, according to proponents of this view, it is an essential aim of social inquiry to come to an understanding of the specific meaningfulness attaching to each

such phenomenon studied. To appreciate the force of this kind
of argument we must, at the outset, attempt to clarify the concept
of meaningfulness. One of the chief difficulties involving this is
that in English, as in several other natural languages, words like
'meaningful' and 'significant' and their cognates occur with a certain systematic ambiguity.

These particular words and their cognates can be used, first,
in a *semantical (nonevaluational)* sense—a sense in which we are explicitly addressing ourselves to the semantical (i.e., referential or
significatory) aspects of language itself. Thus, when we ask "What
is the meaning of the word 'elephant'?" we need not be asking for
an evaluation—in the sense of a judgment about importance—of the
word 'elephant' or its referent. In the second place, there are
many contexts in which our questions about the meanings of things
are not, or not *merely*, inquiries concerning semantical (evaluation-
ally neutral) characteristics. Rather, they are primarily questions
about the importance or value those things may have. It is this
sense of 'meaning' that is at stake when we ask "What is the meaning of (i.e., what is the importance of, or what are important consequences of) France's refusal to sign the test-ban treaty so far as
the Atlantic Alliance is concerned?" or when we assert "The state
visit of Greek royalty to England last year was an empty gesture—
a gesture without meaning."

We are, then, confronted in these arguments with a key word
that is systematically ambiguous; it behooves us therefore to distinguish carefully between the two versions of the arguments as determined by the two meanings of 'meaningful.' To facilitate the
discussion we shall use the term 'meaning$_1$' (or significance$_1$') for
indications of the semantical sense, and 'meaning$_2$' (or signifi-
cance$_2$') for indications of the evaluational sense. In assessing the
arguments we must keep the two senses distinct, even though it is
not always clear that the parties to the controversy have succeeded
in doing so.

Consider first the argument based upon the meaningfulness$_2$,
or significance$_2$, of social phenomena. We may grant at once that
not only do objects and acts that have value or importance come
within the purview of social inquiry, but also that acts *of* valuing
(whether or not such acts have value) are likewise suitable objects
of investigation for the social scientist. The issue that arises is

whether such phenomena necessitate a special methodology for their study. Is there any reason to believe that a hypothesis like (a) 'X is valued or judged to be important by Y' is *logically* impervious to validation through the scientific method?

It is crucial to notice here that this is an issue in the context of validation and not in the context of discovery—it is a question of method or logic or the rationale of validation, and not one of technique of investigation. Incidentally, the Weberian position cannot be construed as merely technological on pain of instant trivialization—it would become simply the uninteresting claim that different techniques need to be employed in different disciplines. On the other hand, from the methodological point of view, the arguments that purport to show that hypotheses like (a) are not amenable to the scientific method of validation, are singularly uncompelling. Generally speaking, these arguments are of two sorts, one being to the effect that value phenomena require that the inquirer himself make a value judgment in order to validate hypotheses concerning their occurrence or some characteristic they may have. The reason advanced to support this claim seems simply to be the presupposition that in order for us to determine, say, that X is regarded as important by Y, or that Y regards X as having some other valuationally relevant characteristic, it is necessary for us, through some empathic act, "to put ourselves in the place of" the evaluating subject of the inquiry. If we do not do this, the argument appears to claim, it will be impossible for us to tell (i.e., to validate the hypothesis) that X is valued, or to ascertain how it is valued.

The second argument, closely related to the first, holds that there is no sort of observable, or empirically testable, *behavior* whose occurrence is both necessary and sufficient for the applicability of any valuational predicates; and that, accordingly, it is impossible to employ the standard validational steps of the scientific method to test hypotheses about valuations .... [T]his amounts to the claim that valuational predicates that occur in social-science theories or hypotheses are not definable by any set of observation predicates, not even introspective or empathic ones.

This last contention, and others related to it, are among the most vexed problems in current analytical philosophy and it would be quite outside the province of this discussion to attempt to settle

it and them here. But we do not have to settle these problems
in order to reject both of the arguments just considered. For the
scientific validation of the types of hypothesis involved is not dependent on the *synonymy* of valuational predicates with any set
of observational (or introspective) ones. All that is required for
scientific validation of the relevant hypothesis is that *some* observable state of affairs be a *likely concomitant* of the value phenomenon in question and not that any observable state of affairs
be both a necessary and sufficient condition for it. To be sure,
in taking the observable concomitant—or its absence—simply as
evidence relevant to the hypothesis, we can never know with certainty whether the hypothesis is true or false; but certainty cannot
attach to the results of *any* empirical inquiry, and our position of
having to accept or reject a valuational hypothesis in the absence
of absolutely conclusive evidence is simply the very condition of
scientific inquiry. (Indeed, one suspects that it is the very urgency
of some atavistic "quest for certainty" in empirical inquiry that
has blinded otherwise perspicacious philosophers and scientists to
this point.) At any rate, here we need neither accept the second
argument that standard validational procedures are inapplicable to
value phenomena nor, a fortiori, the stronger first argument that
some substitute (empathylike) method is indispensable to their
validation. It just *doesn't* take a fat cowherd to drive fat kine!

We have been examining the view that what has been called
the meaning$_2$ of social phenomena necessitates a peculiar methodological divorce of social science from the rest of science. Though
we have not couched the arguments at issue in just the terminology
of Weber's own discussion, the arguments examined (or ones having
substantially their import) do put in an appearance in one guise or
another in his works on the objectivity of social science.

But Weber also seems at times to be arguing from the mean-
ingfulness$_1$ (i.e., semantical meaningfulness) of phenomena to the
same conclusion. And more recently, several extremely acute analytical philosophers, apparently under the influence of Wittgenstein's later writings, have also put forward subtle and profound arguments toward an even more radical (if closely related) conclusion.
The work of Peter Winch . . . is especially challenging.[2]

Winch (and doubtless Weber too) would hold that the concept of a social phenomenon or act must be coextensive with (i.e.,

refer to just the same things as) that of a meaningful$_1$ act. He holds that it is a definitory or essential characteristic of social acts that they should have meaning in what we have been calling the semantical (or significatory) sense of the term.[3] He explicates his use of 'meaningful' (i.e., our 'meaningful$_1$') by equating meaningful behavior with *rule-governed behavior.* He then contends that we must surely fail as students of the character of social phenomena unless we come to understand the meaning$_1$ of such phenomena. Yet, to do this we must understand what it is to behave in conformity with a rule or what it is to "follow a rule." In particular, we must understand what it is to follow the particular rule(s) governing the meaningful$_1$ phenomenon in question.

The explication given by Winch of what it is to follow a rule, is attributed by him to Wittgenstein. Winch tells us that to follow a rule is to act in such a manner that one's action commits one to, and is a sign of commitment to, some further act that it portends and whose nonrealization would presumably constitute a violation of the rule. Rule violation is indeed the key notion involved. We are said to know what it is to follow the rule (and thus, presumably, to "understand" the social phenomena involved) only if we know what would constitute a violation of it. Hence, we know the rule only if we can cogently make judgments of correctness or incorrectness about the act in question.

Having established this much (at least to his own ostensible satisfaction) Winch then raises the question of how an inquirer (or indeed anyone) can come to know or learn what it is to follow a rule, and thus come to know or learn the meaning$_1$ of any social phenomenon. This question brings us to the nub of the matter. For Winch's answer is that the method of science is *wholly irrelevant* to the acquisition of this kind of knowledge; consequently, the scientific method is held to be inappropriate in attempting to consummate the essential task of social science—namely, the task of gaining an understanding of meaningful$_1$ phenomena. It is, according to this view, at best misleading and ineffectual to employ the method used by the rest of the sciences in an area that belongs uniquely to social science. The method Winch claims actually to be appropriate is that of *philosophical analysis* (which for Winch is a task of learning the relevant rules). Sociology (in particular) is thus held by him to be a branch of philosophy rather than an empirical science. The kind of methodology Winch is advocating, would give us, in contrast to the scientific method, just the sort of understanding of the meaning$_1$ of a social act that the subject agent, i.e., the follower of the appropriate rule, himself has.

Now this is a complex argument, and it has ramifications for other areas of philosophy that again cannot appropriately be brought within the scope of this discussion. We are, however, fortunately in a position to assess its worth for our own context without having to explore these extraneous ramifications. . . .

Suppose we were to grant both Winch's contention that all social phenomena are meaningful$_1$ phenomena and also that meaningful$_1$ phenomena are rule-governed phenomena. Even granting this much, Winch's argument seems to fail. Whatever plausibility it has stems from a disguised equivocation over the term 'understanding.' It is hard to cavil at the precept that a social scientist must gain an understanding of the phenomena he investigates, or at the apparent truism that a phenomenon is susceptible of being understood if, and only if, it is intelligible (i.e., understandable). But the next move in Winch's argument, a move that consists in adopting the precept that a meaningful phenomenon is not intelligible or understandable unless its meaning can be understood, makes a pivotal use of the equivocation.

For there are at least two senses of 'understanding' at issue, one of which warrants the application of the term only if the individual to whom it applies has had certain *direct* experiences of the subject matter being "understood." 'Understand,' in the other sense, does not have the occurrence of such experiences as a necessary condition. For example, with respect to the natural sciences it is generally agreed that a scientific understanding or knowledge of things or events of a given kind does not necessarily presuppose direct experience of such things or events. Indeed, as Winch himself points out, we have acquired the understanding appropriate in *natural* science when we have achieved, say, a causal explanation of the type of event being investigated.

Still, there have always been philosophers (Bergson and Whitehead are notable examples) who, while agreeing that causal or scientific explanations of physical phenomena are as much as can be understood by physical science, have nevertheless taken this very fact to be symptomatic of the deficiency or limitations of the scientific method—even as employed in physics. A typical claim maintains that science distorts (through abstraction from) physical reality. It is held, for example, that a scientific description of a tornado conveys in only a feeble, truncated manner what is, on the other hand, conveyed with overpowering richness and fullness by the direct experience of a tornado.

... [T]he shortcomings of this view should be clear. We need but to remember Einstein's remark that it is not the function of science to give the taste of the soup. It is the function of science to describe the world, not to reproduce it. Of course a description of a tornado is *not* the same thing as a tornado! And incidentally, the description does not "fail" to be a tornado on account of being incomplete, truncated, generalized, or abstract. Even if it were a "complete" description of a tornado—whatever that might be—it would still be a *description* of a tornado and not a tornado. Moreover, a description of a tornado no more *fails* to be a tornado than does a tornado fail to be a description.

How, in the end, does all of this bear on Winch's argument? The answer is that Winch's argument commits a rather subtle form of the "reproductive fallacy"—reminding ourselves of the character of the fallacy in the more neutral context of physical science (e.g., illustratively using tornados) allows us to discuss it more easily here.[4] The claim that the only understanding appropriate to social science is one that consists of a reproduction of the conditions or states of affairs being studied, is logically the same as the claim that the only understanding appropriate to the investigation of tornados is that gained in the direct experience of tornados.

We can scarcely entertain the idea that the only kind of understanding at which we can aim in the investigation of tornados must come from the experiencing of tornados. Notice that in rejecting Winch's thesis, it is not necessary to deny that *some sort* of knowledge or understanding of, say, religion is gained in "playing" the "religious game," any more than it is necessary to deny that some sort of knowledge or understanding is gained in experiencing tornados. The point is that nothing whatever in such a concession implies that these direct understandings are either the only ones possible for the social scientist or that they are a substitute for a scientific understanding of social phenomena.[5]

LIBRARY
WEST GEORGIA COLLEGE
CARROLLTON, GEORGIA

Neither Weber's arguments nor the more contemporary but still rather Weberian arguments of Winch are decisive, then, in compelling the conclusion either that social science must fail of achieving the methodological objectivity of the rest of science or that social science must employ a radically distinct methodology.

NOTES

1. On such occasions we may sometimes be invoking the appropriate derivative sense 4 of objectivity; i.e., we may be claiming not only that the sentences of the account are true, but also that the account is not misleading in that it disposes us to believe certain other sentences that are true. Similarly, in claiming that an account is nonobjective, we may be saying that it disposes us to believe certain other sentences that are false.

2. Peter Winch, *The Idea of a Social Science: And Its Relation to Philosophy* (New York: Humanities Press, 1967). [Ed.]

3. For a fuller-scale treatment of the method of science and additional material relevant to the discussion above, see Wesley Salmon, *Logic*, and Carl Hempel, *Philosophy of Natural Science*, in the Prentice-Hall Foundations of Philosophy Series.

4. For a more detailed discussion of Rudner's conception of "the reproductive fallacy," see *Philosophy of Social Science* (Englewood Cliffs, N. J.: Prentice-Hall, 1966), p. 69. [Ed.]

5. For a more detailed discussion of Winch's views and some of their ramifications, see May Brodbeck's "Meaning and Action" in her *Readings in the Philosophy of the Social Sciences* (New York: Macmillan, 1968), pp. 58-78.

4

Objectivity: The Realm of the 'Sacred' in Social Science

Alvin W. Gouldner

. . . There are, it seems to me, at least three . . . possible conceptions of sociological objectivity. One of these can be characterized as "personal authenticity" or "awareness," another can be termed "normative objectification," and the third may be called "transpersonal replicability."

To consider "normative objectification" first: when we talk about the bias or impartiality of a sociologist we are, in effect, talking about the sociologist as if he were a "judge."[1] Now, rendering a judgment premises the existence of conflicting or contending parties; but it does not imply an intention to *mediate* the difficulties between them. The function of a judge is not to bring parties together but is, quite simply, to do justice. Doing justice does not mean, as does mediation or arbitration, that both the parties must each be given or denied a bit of what they sought. Justice does not mean logrolling or "splitting the difference." For the doing of justice may, indeed, give all the benefits to one party and impose all the costs upon another.

From Alvin W. Gouldner, "The Sociologist as Partisan: Sociology and the Welfare State," *The American Sociologist*, 3 (May 1968), pp. 113-116. Copyright © 1968 by The American Sociological Association. Reprinted by permission of The American Sociological Association and the author. The present selection is the concluding section of the original article.

What makes a judgment possessed of justice is not the fact that it distributes costs and benefits equally between the parties but, rather, that the allocation of benefits and costs is made in conformity with some stated normative standard. Justice, in short, is that which is justified in terms of some value. The "impartiality" or objectivity of the judge is an imputation made when it is believed that he has made his decision primarily or solely in terms of some moral value. In one part, then, the objectivity of the judge requires his explication of the moral value in terms of which his judgment has been rendered. One reason why Becker's analysis founders on the problem of objectivity is precisely because it regards the sociologists' value commitment merely as an inescapable fact of nature, rather than viewing it as a necessary condition of his objectivity.[2]

Insofar as the problem [of objectivity] is seen as one of choosing up sides, rather than a working one's way through to a value commitment, I cannot see how it is ever possible for men to recognize that the side to which they are attached can be wrong. But men do not and need not always say, "my country right or wrong." Insofar as they are capable of distinguishing the side to which they are attached, from the *grounds* on which they are attached to it, they are, to that extent, capable of a significant objectivity.

It should again be clear, then, that I do not regard partisanship as incompatible with objectivity. The physician, after all, is not necessarily less objective because he has made a partisan commitment to his patient and against the germ. The physician's objectivity is in some measure vouchsafed because he has committed himself to a specific value: health. It is this commitment that constrains him to see and to say things about the patient's condition that neither may want to know.

But in saying that the explication of the sociologist's value commitment is a necessary condition for his objectivity, we are saying little unless we recognize at the same time the grinding difficulties involved in this. For one, it is no easy thing to know what our own value commitments are. In an effort to seem frank and open, we all too easily pawn off a merely glib statement about our values without making any effort to be sure that these are the values to which we are actually committed. This is much of what

happens when scientists conventionally assert that they believe
only in "the truth." Secondly, a mere assertion of a value commitment is vainly ritualistic to the extent that the sociologist has
no awareness of the way in which one of his commitments may
conflict with or exclude another. For example, there is commonly some tension between a commitment to truth and a commitment to welfare. Third, we also have to recognize that the values
in terms of which we may make our judgments may not necessarily
be shared by the participants in the situations we have studied.
Our objectivity, however, does not require us to share values with
those we study, but only to apply the values that we claim are our
own, however unpopular these may be. In other words, this form
of objectivity requires that we be on guard against our own hypocrisy and our need to be loved. This creates a problem because the
values we may actually hold may differ from those we feel that we
must display in order to gain or maintain access to research sites.

To come to another meaning of sociological objectivity,
"personal authenticity." If the previous conception of objectivity, "normative objectification," emphasizes that the sociologist
must not deceive *others* concerning the value basis of his judgment, then personal authenticity stresses that the sociologist must
not deceive *himself* concerning the basis of his judgment. By personal authenticity or awareness, I mean to call attention to the relationship between the sociologist's beliefs about the actual state
of the social world, on the one hand, and his own personal wishes,
hopes, and values for this social world, on the other hand. Personal authenticity or awareness exists when the sociologist is capable
of admitting the factuality even of things that violate his own
hopes and values. People do differ in this regard, some having a
greater capacity and need for self-deception and others possessing
less talent to attain the comforts born of such self-deception. Not
all conservatives are equally blind to the fragility of the *status quo*;
not all radicals are equally blind to its stability.

In this sense, then, one form of sociological objectivity involves the capacity to acknowledge "hostile information"—information that is discrepant with our purposes, hopes, wishes, or
values. It is not the state of the world, then, that makes information hostile, but only the state of the world in relation to a
man's wants and values. Here, then, objectivity consists in the

capacity to know and to use—to seek out, or at least to accept it when it is otherwise provided—information inimical to our own desires and values, and to overcome our own fear of such information.

Both forms of objectivity imply a paradoxical condition: namely, that one cannot be objective about the world outside without, to some extent, being knowledgeable about (and in control of) ourselves. In normative objectification, one of the central problems is to *know* our values, and to see that such knowledge is problematic. In personal authenticity there is a need for a similar knowledge of the self, but for a knowledge that goes beyond values into the question of our brute impulses and of other desires or wants that we may not at all feel to be valuable. In both forms of objectivity, also, it would be foolhardy to expect that the requisite knowledge is acquirable through a simple process of frictionless "retrieval." Rather, we must expect that either form of objectivity entails some measure of *struggle* in and with the sociologist's self and, with this, a need for courage. It now should be clear why I have taken up the cudgels against complacency, for it is the very antithesis of the kind of moral struggle required for objectivity.

Insofar as the pursuit of objectivity rests upon what I must reluctantly call "moral character," we can also see another source from which sociological objectivity is deeply undermined today. It is undermined, from one direction, by a compulsive and exclusive cultivation of purely technical standards of research and of education, so that there is neither a regard nor a locus of responsibility for the cultivation of those very moral qualities on which objectivity rests. The truth is that to the extent that sociology and sociological education remain obsessed with a purely technical focus they have abdicated a concern with objectivity; it is merely hypocritical for those with such a standpoint to enter occasional accusations about other's lack of objectivity.

A second basic inner locus for our default with respect to the problem of objectivity is the growing transformation of sociology into a profession. This may seem paradoxical again, for surely professions profess value commitments, at least to client, if not public, welfare. Professions, however, do not tend to see value commitments as questions of personal commitment but tend, instead, simply to treat the values they transmit as non-problematic givens. Most civic professions tend to take the larger culture and institutions in their society as given. But it is precisely the peculiar nature of the sociologist's task to be able to take them as problematic. The development of professionalization among sociologists deserves to be opposed because it undermines the sociologist's capacity for *objectivity* in any serious sense. In effect, the growth of professionalization means the substitution of a routine and banal code of ethics for a concern with the serious kind of morality on which alone objectivity might rest.

A third specific conception of objectivity common to many American sociologists—and so common, in fact, that even C. Wright Mills agreed with it—is what has been termed "transpersonal replicability." In this notion, objectivity simply means that a sociologist has described his procedures with such explicitness that others employing them on the same problem will come to the same conclusion. In effect, then, this is a notion of objectivity as technical routinization and rests, at bottom, on the codification and explication of the research procedures that were employed. At most, however, this is an *operational* definition of objectivity which presumably tells us what we must *do* in order to justify an assertion that some particular finding is objective. It does not, however, tell us very much about what objectivity *means* conceptually and connotatively. It says only that those findings which are replicated are to be considered to be objective.

It is quite possible, however, that any limited empirical generalization can, by this standard, be held to be objective, however narrow, partial, or biased and prejudiced its net impact is, by reason of its selectivity. Thus, for example, one might conduct research into the occupational-political distribution of Jews and come to the conclusion that a certain proportion of them are bankers and Communists. Given the replicability conception of objectivity, one might then simply claim that this (subsequently verified) finding is "objective," and this claim could be made legitimately even though one never compared the proportions of bankers and Communists among Jews with those among Protestants and Catholics. It might be said that, without such a comparison among the three religions, one would never know whether the proportion of bankers and Communists among Jews was higher or lower than that among

Protestants and Catholics. But this objection would simply indicate the technical statistical condition that must be met in order to justify a statement concerning the Jewish *differential*. Insofar as one happens not to be interested in making or justifying a statement about this, the objectivity of the original statement remains defensible in terms of the technical conception of objectivity as replicability. Thus it would seem that the replicability criterion falls far short of what is commonly implied by objectivity.

This technical conception of objectivity is in part, but in part only, reminiscent of the manner in which Max Weber conceived of it. We might say that the current conception is a kind of mindless corruption of Weber's. Weber essentially thought of scientific objectivity as something left over. It was a residual sphere of the purely technical, a realm in which decisions should and could be made without thought of their ultimate value relevancies. Weber's approach to objectivity comes down to a strategy of segregation—the conscientious maintenance of a strict separation between the world of facts and the world of values. Weber's emphasis here, therefore, is not on the manner in which scientific objectivity depends upon value commitments; this tends tacitly to be assumed rather than deliberately insisted upon. Weber's stress is placed, rather, upon the separation and discontinuity of facts and values. As a result, one may come away believing that, to Weber, the objectivity of research need not be colored by the scientist's personal values or the manner in which these are arrived at and held. *En principe*, neither the sanity nor maturity of a scientist need affect his objectivity. The madman and the teenager can be as scientifically objective as anyone else in this view, so long as they adhere to purely technical standards of science, once having committed themselves to some problem. Weber's theory invites a fantasy that objectivity may, at some point, be surrendered entirely to the impersonal machinery of research.

The passionate artfulness with which Weber argues this case endows the world that he conjures in imagination to be mistaken for reality, and we may fail to notice just how *grotesque* this conjured world is. Actually, Weber's entire enterprise here is born of his attempt to overcome his conception of the world as grotesque by formulating a salvational myth of a value-free social science. Through this he strives to still his furious sense of uneasiness that the real world, in which science and morality do cohabit, is a world of mutually destructive incompatibles. Weber fantasies a solution in which facts and values will each be preserved in watertight compartments. The tensions and dangers of the conjunction of facts and values are to be overcome by a segregation of the sequential phases of research, so that: first, the scientist formulates his problem in terms of his value interests and, then, having done this, he puts his values behind him, presumably never again allowing them to intrude into the subsequent stage of technical analysis.

To overcome his experience of the world as grotesque, Weber formulates an incipient utopia in which the impure world is split into two pure worlds, science and morality. He then attempts to bridge the cleavage he has created by pasting these two purified worlds together, so that each is made sovereign in a different but adjacent period of time. The incongruity of the world has not so much been overcome as transcended in myth. The experienced unmanageability of the one world gives way to the promised manageability of the two worlds. The reality gives way to the myth, but the grotesqueness abides.

One central difference between Weber's and the current technical conception of objectivity is that Weber recognized that the technical sphere would have to be brought into some sort of alignment with the value sphere. The modern technical conception of objectivity, however, simply regards the value problem and its relation to the technical as either negligible or dull. It allows it to remain unclarified. The modern technical approach to objectivity also differs from the Weberian in a second way. The former takes it for granted that, somehow, social scientists will do the right thing. It assumes that, in some manner, there will be a mustering of motives sufficient to make social scientists conform with their technical standards and rules.

Commonly, the source of these motives is not explored. Sometimes, however, it is today held that the mutual inspection and the checks and balances of modern *professionalization* will suffice to keep social scientists honest. In short, it is assumed that the machinery of professionalism will make the machinery of science work.

This expectation underestimates the ease with which professionalism is corruptible as well as the power of the corrupting forces. Perhaps the most important example of this in the present generation was the work of the Warren Commission appointed by President Lyndon Johnson to investigate the assassination of President John Kennedy. Whatever one's conclusions concerning the substantive issues, namely, whether Lee Harvey Oswald was the assassin, and whether or not he alone or in conspiracy with others murdered President Kennedy, one miserable conclusion seems unavoidable: that there was scarcely a civic profession—the military, the medical, the police, the legal, the juridical—that was not involved in suppressing or distorting the truth, and which did not bow obsequiously to power. And I am far from sure that this was always motivated by a concern for the national welfare. The more that the respectable professions are transformed from independent vocations into bureaucratic and federally sponsored dependencies the more corruptible they will be in the future. Those who think that professional associations and universities will immunize the professions from the pressures and temptations of power have simply not understood the revelations about the CIA penetration into these very associations and universities. For these show that they were willing and eager parties to their own corruption in the name of a well-financed patriotic devotion.

For his part, however, Weber never assumed that the technical machinery of science would be self-winding and self-maintaining. For Weber, the maintenance of objectivity at least required a persisting moral effort to prevent one's personal values from intruding into purely technical decisions. The machinery was really never thought of as operating successfully apart from men's characters. Weber premises that, even in the purely technical stages of later research, work will be subject to an ongoing superintendence by the social scientist's moral commitment to "truth." Since the continued force of this personal value is conceived to be compatible with the maintenance of technical standards, its significance is left unexplicated. It is only implicitly, therefore, that Weber indicates that the objectivity of research depends continuingly, and not only in the early problem-formulating stages, upon something more than the technical machinery of research.

The question arises, however, as to the meaning of this extra-technical, "transcendental" commitment to the truth. Does it entail anything more than a commitment to the segregation of facts and values? Either it has some meaning beyond this or it does not. If it does not, then we are still left wondering how and why social scientists may be relied upon to adhere to this very segregation of facts and values: What endows it with binding force? If it does, and if the "truth" that it demands is something more than the mere application of technical standards alone, then it must entail something more than a belief in reliability or validity. If "truth" is not merely a summarizing redundancy for these terms it must be embedded with some conception that embodies or resonates value commitments that call for something more than pure truth alone.

The pursuit of "truth for its own sake" is always a tacit quest for something more than truth, for other values that may have been obscured, denied, and perhaps even forbidden, and some of which are expressed in the quest for "objectivity." Objectivity expresses a lingering attachment to something more than the purely technical goods of science alone and for more than the valid-reliable bits of information it may produce. In this sense, "truth for its own sake" is a crypto-ethic, a concealment of certain other substantive values through a strategy that, leaving them entirely in the open, diverts attention from them to another dramatically accentuated valuable: truth. The old Druidic sacred place is not destroyed; it is merely housed in an imposing new cathedral. In affirming that he only seeks the truth for its own sake, the scientist is therefore not so much lying as pledging allegiance to the flag of truth, while saying nothing about the country for which it stands.

What are the other values that lie obscured in the long shadows cast by the light of pure truth? In Western culture, these often enough have been freedom—the truth will set you free—and power —to know, in order to control. Underlying the conception of truth as objectivity there is, however, still another value, a faint but enduring image of the possibility of *wholeness*. One obvious implication of objectivity has commonly been to tell the "whole" story. The longing here is to fit the partial and broken fragments together; to provide a picture that transcends the nagging sense of incompleteness; to overcome the multiplicity of shifting perspectives. Underlying the quest for objectivity, then, is the hope of dissolving the differences that divide and the distances that separate men by uniting them in a single, peace-bringing vision of the world.

In such a conception of objectivity there is, I suspect, the undertow of an illicit yearning that links science to religion. Perhaps this conclusion is an illusion. Worse still, perhaps it is "sentimental." Yet it will not seem so fanciful if it is remembered that the modern conception of an objective social science was born with early nineteenth century Positivism. This set itself the task of creating both an objective social science and a new religion of humanity, each informing the other and aimed at reuniting society. The objectivity of the new sociology was, from its very beginnings, not an end in itself; it was clearly aimed at the enhancement of human unity and it then had the most intimate connection with an openly religious impulse.

The conception of objectivity has commonly projected an image of the scientist as linked to a higher realm, as possessed of a godlike penetration into things, as serenely above human frailties and distorting passions, or as possessed of a priest-like impartiality. The realm of objectivity is the higher realm of *episteme*, of *wahrheit*, of *raison*, of Truth, which have always been something more than sheer information. In other words, the realm of objectivity is the realm of the *sacred* in social science. But why has the quest for this realm been encrusted under the defensive conception of truth for its own sake?

Essentially the fate of objectivity in sociology is linked with, and its fortunes vary with, the changing hopes for a peace-bringing human unity. Some power-tempted social scientists are simply no longer able to hear this music. Others may withdraw because their hope is so vital that they cannot risk endangering it by an open confrontation. For some, an open admission would be dissonant with their conception of themselves as tough-minded and hardheaded. Still others have a genuine humility and feel that the pursuit of this high value is beyond their powers. There are also some who doubt the very value of peace itself because, oddly enough, they want men to endure and to live, and they suspect that the successful quest for a peace-bringing unity spells death: they ask themselves, after unity and peace, what?

Perhaps what has been most discrediting to the quest for human unity is that, since its classical formulation, its most gifted spokesmen have often had totalitarian proclivities; they came to be viewed as enemies of the "open society," who denied the value and reality of human difference. In short, the plea for human unity has often, and quite justifiably, been interpreted as a demand for a tension-free society that was overseen by a close superintendence of men from nursery to graveyard, and was blanketed with a re-morseless demand for conformity and consensus. What has really been discredited, however, was this chilling version of the dream of human unity, although it remains extremely difficult to extri-cate the larger hope from the nightmare form that it was given.

Whether objectivity is thought possible comes down then to a question of whether some vision of human unity is believed workable and desirable. It comes down to the question, as C. Wright Mills once said, of whether there is still some vision of a larger "public" whose interests and needs transcend those of its component and contending factions. In this sense, one possible meaning of objectivity in social science is the contribution it might make to a human unity of mankind. But to make such a contribu-tion the social sciences cannot and should not be impartial toward human suffering; they must not make their peace with any form of human unity that complacently accommodates itself to or im-poses suffering.

At the same time, however, an empty-headed partisanship unable to transcend the immediacies of narrowly conceived politi-cal commitment is simply just one more form of market research. A blind or unexamined alliance between sociologists and the upper bureaucracy of the welfare state can only produce the market re-search of liberalism. It rests upon the tacit, mistaken, but com-mon, liberal assumption that the policies of this bureaucracy equi-tably embody the diverse interests of the larger public, rather than seeing that the bureaucracy is one other interested and powerful contending faction, and is more closely allied with some of the contenders rather than equally distant from all. It is to values, not to factions, that sociologists must give their most basic commit-ment.

NOTES

1. The next paragraph or so is indebted to the excellent discus-sion by Rostein Eckhoff, "The Mediator, the Judge and the Admin-istrator in Conflict-Resolution," *Acta Sociologica*, Vol. 10, pp. 148-172.

2. The reader should be aware that "The Sociologist as Partisan: Sociology and the Welfare State" (the essay from which the present selection was extracted) is a caustic and at times brilliant response to the sociologist Howard S. Becker's "Whose Side Are We On?", a paper that is reprinted below. Although Professor Gouldner agrees with Becker that partisanship is unavoidable in sociological research, he criticizes him for (1) failure to make clear "whose side he (Becker) is on" and (2) excessive complacency with respect to the compatibility of partisan research in sociology and objective research. For Gouldner's discussion of this last point, see "The Sociologist as Partisan: Sociology and the Welfare Stage," *The American Sociologist*, 3 (May 1968), pp. 110-113. [Ed.]

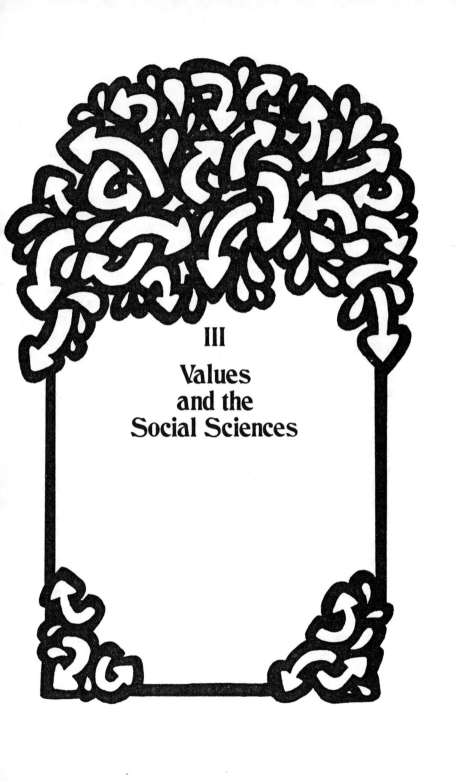

III

Values
and the
Social Sciences

Max Weber's (1864-1920) thoughts on the role of values in social scientific research are, if not contradictory, at least complex. On the one hand, he was a vigorous advocate of a *value-free* social science. Although social scientists must seek to understand the values involved in the actions or institutions they are studying, Weber stresses that it is not part of social scientists' task (qua scientists) to express either approval or disapproval of these values. Seek to understand the values held in society, yes! Advocate a personal value commitment, no! On the other hand, Weber held that social scientists study only that subject matter to which they attribute "cultural significance." Consequently, a *value orientation* is inherent in the choice of material for social scientific investigation. To quote Weber, "The concept of culture is a *value-concept.* Empirical reality becomes 'culture' to us because and insofar as we relate it to value ideas. It includes those segments and only those segments of reality which have become significant to us because of this value-relevance." (Weber, 1949, p. 76)

The complexity of Weber's thoughts on values will not be reflected in the selection contained in this volume. For this, the reader should consult the essays published under the title *The Methodology of the Social Sciences.* What have been selected for publication here are those parts of " 'Objectivity' in Social Science and Social Policy" and a brief passage from "The Meaning of 'Ethical Neutrality' " that contain Weber's reasons for advocating the value-free status of the social sciences.

The occasion of Weber's expressing himself on this topic was his assumption, along with Werner Sombart and Edgar Jaffé, of the editorship of the *Archiv fuer Sozialwissenschaft und Sozialpolitik.* The year was 1904. As the new editor, Weber thought it important to state clearly the editorial policy that he and his associates would follow. Such a statement was especially urgent, Weber thought, in light of his intention to continue publishing two kinds of papers: (1) papers that would extend man's knowledge of the "facts of social life" and (2) papers that would *criticize* existing social policies and *recommend* new ones. The dual thrust of the *Archiv,* therefore, raised the issue of the relationship between values and social scientific knowledge.

The key to Weber's position is the sharp distinction he draws between two kinds of knowledge: "existential knowledge" and "normative knowledge." The differences between the two can be summarized as follows: (1) The former refers to knowledge of "what is"; the latter to knowledge of what "should be." (2) The former provides answers to *scientific (causal) questions* (e.g., What are the economic, social, etc., variables that can be manipulated in order either to impede or to foment revolutionary activity in underdeveloped countries?); the latter provides answers to *policy questions* (e.g., Ought the United States to engage in counterinsurgency activity in Southeast Asia?). (3) The former is the subject matter for "rational and empirical" investigation; the latter the subject matter of "faith." (4) The former is objective in the sense of not being culturally determined; the latter is nonobjective in the sense of being culturally relative. (5) Existential knowledge is concerned with "means," normative knowledge with "ends." And finally, (6) it is the task of the social sciences to provide the former, the task of individual choice to determine the latter. Once these differences are noted, Weber believes that the boundaries of social science have been correctly demarcated and the sense in which the social sciences are value-free has been defined. Although the social sciences can (and must) be value-free, Weber does not consider this fact to be an argument for moral indifference on the part of individual scientists. Rather, the argument is simply that social science's task is to tell us what we *can* do, not what we *ought* to do.

Abraham Kaplan, the distinguished philosopher from the University of Michigan, argues in "Values in Inquiry" that "not all value concerns are unscientific, that indeed some of them are called for by the scientific enterprise itself, and that those which run counter to scientific ideals can be brought under control." Unlike Weber, therefore, Kaplan maintains that the social sciences cannot be value-free; but like Alvin Gouldner, he thinks that a value-laden science can be objective. Kaplan holds the former view because of his belief that in the social sciences values (1) compose much of the subject matter to be investigated; (2) constitute the ethics of the profession — for example, reliance on evidence, openness to counterevidence, and the passion for truth; (3) serve as the basis for the selection of problems; and (4) determine both the *meaning* of social events and what constitutes a social *fact*. Nevertheless, an objective social science is possible — and for two reasons. First, the points at which values enter social scientific inquiry do not necessarily make for bias. Thus, even though values compose much of the subject matter to be investigated, it is their existence, not their validity, that is of interest to the social scientist. Furthermore, the values that define the ethics of the profession work "to eradicate bias, or at least to minimize it and to mitigate its effects." And finally, insofar as values only dictate problems, rather than prejudge solutions, they pose no difficulty in serving as the basis for selecting topics to be studied. Kaplan draws his second reason for considering an objective social science possible from his belief that values can be "empirically grounded." So long as values are not necessarily and irreducibly subjective, they can determine social facts and social meaning without jeopardizing the social sciences' claim on objectivity. In the final analysis, Kaplan is wary of attempts to protect values *from* science because they sacrifice the possibility of supporting values *by* science. This is the danger of succumbing to the call for a value-free social science.

A vast amount of interpretative literature on the thought of Max Weber exists. Of special interest are the following: Dahrendorf (1968); Gouldner (1962; 1968); Horowitz (1962); Parsons (1967); and Nagel (1961), Ch. 13. For an argument in support of distinguishing scientific (causal) questions from policy questions, see Passmore (1953).

The literature on values in the social sciences is no less extensive. Like Kaplan, Roshwald (1955) argues that since values can be empirically established, a value-laden social science poses no threat to an objective social science. In addition, see Braybrooke (1958); Eister (1964); Eulau (1968); Furfey (1959); Golightly (1956); Gunther and Reshaur (1971); Klappholz (1964); Köhler (1938); Levi (1960); Myrdal (1944); Nagel (1961) and Mackenzie's (1967) reply to Nagel; and Rudner (1953). Finally, with respect to Kaplan's belief that values determine social facts and social meaning, compare Kuhn (1970), Chs. 9 and 10, as well as Scheffler (1967).

5

"Objectivity" in Social Science and Social Policy

Max Weber

When a social science journal which also at times concerns itself with a social policy, appears for the first time or passes into the hands of a new editorial board, it is customary to ask about its "line." We, too, must seek to answer this question, and . . . we will enter into the question in a more fundamental theoretical way. Even though or perhaps because, we are concerned with "self-evident truths," this occasion provides the opportunity to cast some light on the nature of the "social sciences" as we understand them, in such a manner that it can be useful, if not to the specialist, then to the reader who is more remote from actual scientific work.

In addition to the extension of our knowledge of the "social conditions of all countries," i.e., the facts of social life, the express purpose of the *Archiv* ever since its establishment has been the education of judgment about practical social problems — and in the very modest way in which such a goal can be furthered by private scholars — the criticism of practical social policy, extending even

Reprinted with permission of The Macmillan Company from *The Methodology of the Social Sciences* by Max Weber, translated and edited by Edward A. Shils and Henry A. Finch. Copyright © 1949 by The Free Press. The present article consists of excerpts from " 'Objectivity' in Social Science and Social Policy," pp. 50-61, and from "The Meaning of 'Ethical Neutrality'," pp. 18-21.

as far as legislation. In spite of this, the *Archiv* has firmly adhered, from the very beginning, to its intention to be an exclusively scientific journal and to proceed only with the methods of scientific research. Hence arises the question of whether the purpose stated above is compatible in principle with self-confinement to the latter method. What has been the meaning of the value-judgments found in the pages of the *Archiv* regarding legislative and administrative measures, or practical recommendations for such measures? What are the standards governing these judgments? What is the validity of the value-judgments which are uttered by the critic, for instance, or on which a writer recommending a policy founds his arguments for that policy? In what sense, if the criterion of scientific knowledge is to be found in the "objective" validity of its results, has he remained within the sphere of *scientific* discussion? We will first present our own attitude on this question in order later to deal with the broader one: in what sense are there in general "objectively valid truths" in those disciplines concerned with social and cultural phenomena? This question, in view of the continuous changes and bitter conflict about the apparently most elementary problems of our discipline, its methods, the formulation and validity of its concepts, cannot be avoided. We do not attempt to offer solutions but rather to disclose problems — problems of the type to which our journal, if it is to meet its past and future responsibilities, must turn its attention.

We all know that our science, as is the case with every science treating the institutions and events of human culture, (with the possible exception of political history) first arose in connection with *practical* considerations. Its most immediate and often sole purpose was the attainment of value-judgments concerning measures of State economic policy. It was a "technique" in the same sense as, for instance, the clinical disciplines in the medical sciences are. It has now become known how this situation was gradually modified. This modification was not, however, accompanied by a formulation of the logical (*prinzipielle*) distinction between "existential knowledge," i.e., knowledge of what "is," and "normative knowledge," i.e., knowledge of what "should be." The formulation of this distinction was hampered, first, by the view that immutably invariant natural laws, — later, by the view that an unambiguous evolutionary principle — governed economic life and that accordingly, *what was normatively right* was identical — in the former case — with the immutably *existent* — and in the latter — with the inevitably *emergent*. With the awakening of the historical sense, a combination of ethical evolutionism and historical relativism became the predominant attitude in our science. This attitude sought to deprive ethical norms of their formal character and through the incorporation of the totality of cultural values into the "ethical" (*Sittlichen*) sphere tried to give a *substantive content* to ethical norms. It was hoped thereby to raise economics to the status of an "ethical science" with empirical foundations. To the extent that an "ethical" label was given to all possible cultural ideals, the particular autonomy of the ethical imperative was obliterated, without however increasing the "objective" validity of those ideals. Nonetheless we can and must forego a discussion of the principles at issue. We merely point out that even today the confused opinion that economics does and should derive value-judgments from a specifically "economic point of view" has not disappeared but is especially current, quite understandably, among men of practical affairs.

Our journal as the representative of an empirical specialized discipline must, as we wish to show shortly, reject this view in principle. It must do so because, in our opinion, it can never be the task of an empirical science to provide binding norms and ideals from which directives for immediate practical activity can be derived.

What is the implication of this proposition? It is certainly not that value-judgments are to be withdrawn from scientific discussion in general simply because in the last analysis they rest on certain ideals and are therefore "subjective" in origin. Practical action and the aims of our journal would always reject such a proposition. Criticism is not to be suspended in the presence of value-judgments. The problem is rather: what is the meaning and purpose of the scientific criticism of ideals and value-judgments? This requires a somewhat more detailed analysis.

All serious reflection about the ultimate elements of meaningful human conduct is oriented primarily in terms of the categories "end" and "means." We desire something concretely either "for its own sake" or as a means of achieving something else which is more highly desired. The question of the appropriateness of the means for achieving a given end is undoubtedly accessible to scientific analysis. Inasmuch as we are able to determine (within the present limits of our knowledge) which means for the achievement of a proposed end are appropriate or inappropriate, we can in this way estimate the chances of attaining a certain end by certain available means. In this way we can indirectly criticize the setting of the end itself as practically meaningful (on the basis of the existing historical situation) or as meaningless with reference to existing conditions. Furthermore, when the possibility of attaining a proposed end appears to exist, we can determine (naturally within the limits of our existing knowledge) the consequences which the application of the means to be used will produce in addition to the eventual attainment of the proposed end, as a result of the interdependence of all events. We can then provide the acting person with the ability to weigh and compare the undesirable as over against the desirable consequences of his action. Thus, we can answer the question: what will the attainment of a desired end "cost" in terms of the predictable loss of other values? Since, in the vast majority of cases, every goal that is striven for does "cost" or can "cost" something in this sense, the weighing of the goal in terms of the incidental consequences of the action which realizes it cannot be omitted from the deliberation of persons who act with a sense of responsibility. One of the most important functions of the *technical criticism* which we have been discussing thus far is to make this sort of analysis possible. To apply the results of this analysis in the making of a decision, however, is not a task which science can undertake; it is rather the task of the acting, willing person: he weighs and chooses from among the values involved according to his own conscience and his personal view of the world. Science can make him realize that all action and naturally, according to the circumstances, inaction imply in their consequences the espousal of certain values — and herewith — what is today so willingly overlooked — the rejection of certain others. The act of choice itself is his own responsibility.

We can also offer the person, who makes a choice, insight into the significance of the desired object. We can teach him to think in terms of the context and the meaning of the ends he desires, and among which he chooses. We do this through making explicit and developing in a logically consistent manner the "ideas" which actually do or which can underlie the concrete end. It is self-evident that one of the most important tasks of every science of cultural life is to arrive at a rational understanding of these "ideas" for which men either really or allegedly struggle. This does not overstep the boundaries of a science which strives for an "analytical ordering of empirical reality," although the methods which are used in this interpretation of cultural (*geistiger*) values are not "inductions" in the usual sense. At any rate, this task falls at least partly beyond the limits of economics as defined according to the conventional division of labor. It belongs among the tasks of social philosophy. However, the historical influence of ideas in the development of social life has been and still is so great that our journal cannot renounce this task. It shall rather regard the investigation of this phenomenon as one of its most important obligations.

But the scientific treatment of value-judgments may not only understand and empathically analyze (*nacherleben*) the desired ends and the ideals which underlie them; it can also "judge" them critically. This criticism can of course have only a dialetical character, i.e., it can be no more than a formal logical judgment of historically given value-judgments and ideas, a testing of the ideals according to the postulate of the internal *consistency* of the desired end. It can, insofar as it sets itself this goal, aid the acting willing person in attaining self-clarification concerning the final axioms from which his desired ends are derived. It can assist him in becoming aware of the ultimate standards of value which he does not make explicit to himself or, which he must presuppose in order to be logical. The elevation of these ultimate standards, which are manifested in concrete value-judgments, to the level of explicitness is the utmost that the scientific treatment of value-judgments can do without entering into the realm of speculation. As to whether the person expressing these value-judgments *should* adhere to these ultimate standards is his personal affair; it involves will and conscience, not empirical knowledge.

An empirical science cannot tell anyone what he *should* do — but rather what he *can* do — and under certain circumstances — what he wishes to do. It is true that in our sciences, personal value-judgments have tended to influence scientific arguments without being explicitly admitted. They have brought about continual confusion and have caused various interpretations to be placed on scientific arguments even in the sphere of the determination of simple casual interconnections among facts according to whether the results increased or decreased the chances of realizing one's personal ideals, i.e., the possibility of desiring a certain thing. Even the editors and the collaborators of our journal will regard "nothing human as alien" to them in this respect. But it is a long way from this acknowledgement of human frailty to the belief in an "ethical" science of economics, which would derive ideals from its subject matter and produce concrete norms by applying general ethical imperatives. It is true that we regard as *objectively* valuable those innermost elements of the "personality," those highest and most ultimate value-judgments which determine our conduct and give meaning and significance to our life. We can indeed espouse these values only when they appear to us as valid, as derived from our highest values and when they are developed in the struggle against the difficulties which life presents. Certainly, the dignity of the "personality" lies in the fact that for it there exist values about which it organizes its life; — even if these values are in certain cases concentrated exclusively within the sphere of the person's "individuality," then "self-realization" in *those* interests for which it claims *validity* as *values,* is the idea with respect to which its whole existence is oriented. Only on the assumption of belief in the validity of values is the attempt to espouse value-judgments meaningful. However, to *judge* the *validity* of such values is a matter of *faith.* It may perhaps be a task for the speculative interpretation of life and the universe in quest of their meaning. But it certainly does not fall within the province of an empirical science in the sense in which it is to be practised here. The empirically demonstrable fact that these ultimate ends undergo historical changes and are debatable does not affect this distinction between empirical science and value-judgments, contrary to what is often thought. For even the knowledge of the most certain proposition of our theoretical sciences — e.g., the exact natural sciences or mathematics, is, like the cultivation and refinement of the conscience, a product of culture. However, when we call to mind the practical problems of economic and social policy (in the usual sense), we see that there are many, indeed countless, practical questions in the discussion of which there seems to be general agreement about the self-evident character of certain goals. Among these we may mention emergency credit, the concrete problems of social hygiene, poor relief, factory inspection, industrial courts, employment exchanges, large sections of protective labor legislation — in short, all those issues in which, at least in appearance, only the *means* for the attainment of the goal are at issue. But even if we were to mistake the illusion of self-evidence for truth — which science can never do without damaging itself — and wished to view the conflicts immediately arising from attempts at practical realization as purely technical questions of expediency — which would very often be incorrect — even in this case we would have to recognize that this illusion of the self-evidence of normative standards of value is dissipated as soon as we pass from the concrete problems of philanthropic and protective social and economic services to problems of economic and social policy. The distinctive characteristic of a problem of social *policy* is indeed the fact that it cannot be resolved merely on the basis of purely technical considerations which assume already settled ends. Normative standards of value can and must be the objects of *dispute* in a discussion of a problem of social policy because the problem lies in the domain of general *cultural* values. And the conflict occurs not merely, as we are too easily inclined to believe today, between "class interests" but between general views on life and the universe as well. This latter point, however, does not lessen the truth that the particular ultimate value-judgment which the individual espouses is decided among other factors and certainly to a quite significant degree by the degree of affinity between it and his class interests — accepting for the time being this only superficially unambiguous term. One thing is certain under all circumstances, namely, the more "general" the problem involved, i.e., in this case, the broader its cultural *significance*, the less subject it is to a single unambiguous answer on the basis of the data of empirical sciences and the greater the role played by value-ideas (*Wertideen*) and the ultimate and highest personal axioms of belief. It is simply naive to believe, although there are many specialists who even now occasionally do, that it is possible to establish and to demonstrate as scientifically valid "a principle" for practical social science from which the norms for the solution of practical problems can be unambiguously derived. However much the social sciences need the discussion of practical problems in terms of fundamental principles, i.e., the reduction of unreflective value-judgments to the premises from which they are logically derived and however much our journal intends to devote itself specially to them — certainly the creation of a lowest common denominator for our problems in the form of generally valid ultimate value-judgments cannot be its task or in general the task of any empirical science. Such a thing would not only be impracticable; it would be entirely meaningless as well. Whatever the interpretation of the basis and the nature of the validity of the ethical imperatives, it is certain that from them, as from the norms for the concretely conditioned conduct of the *individual, cultural values* cannot be unambiguously derived as being normatively desirable; it can do so the less, the more inclusive are the values concerned. Only positive religions — or more precisely expressed: dogmatically bound *sects* — are able to confer on the content of *cultural values* the status of unconditionally valid *ethical* imperatives. Outside these sects, cultural ideals which the individual wishes to realize and ethical obligations which he *should* fulfil do not, in principle, share the same status. The fate of an epoch which has eaten of the tree of knowledge is that it must know that we cannot learn the *meaning* of the world from the results of its analysis, be it ever so perfect; it must rather be in a position to create this meaning itself. It must recognize that general views of life and the universe can never be the products of increasing empirical knowledge, and that the highest ideals, which move us most forcefully, are always formed only in the struggle with other ideals which are just as sacred to others as ours are to us.

Only an optimistic syncretism, such as is, at times, the product of evolutionary-historical relativism, can theoretically delude itself about the profound seriousness of this situation or practically shirk its consequences. It can, to be sure, be just as obligatory subjectively for the practical politician, in the individual case, to mediate between antagonistic points of view as to take sides with one of them. But this has nothing whatsoever to do with scientific "objectivity." *Scientifically the "middle course" is not truer even by a hair's breadth,* than the most extreme party ideals of the right or left. Nowhere are the interests of science more poorly served in the long run than in those situations where one refuses to see uncomfortable facts and the realities of life in all their starkness. The *Archiv* will struggle relentlessly against the severe self-deception which asserts that through the synthesis of several party points of view, or by following a line between them, practical norms of *scientific validity* can be arrived at. It is necessary to do this because, since this piece of self-deception tries to mask its own standards of value in relativistic terms, it is more dangerous to the freedom of research than the former naive faith of parties in the scientific "demonstrability" of their dogmas. The capacity to distinguish between empirical knowledge and value-judgments, and the fulfillment of the scientific duty to see the factual truth as well as the practical duty to stand up for our own ideals constitute the program to which we wish to adhere with ever increasing firmness.

There is and always will be — and this is the reason that it concerns us — an unbridgeable distinction among (1) those arguments which appeal to our capacity to become enthusiastic about and our feeling for concrete practical aims or cultural forms and values, (2) those arguments in which, once it is a question of the validity of ethical norms, the appeal is directed to our conscience, and finally (3) those arguments which appeal to our capacity and need for *analytically ordering* empirical reality in a manner which lays claim to *validity* as empirical truth. This proposition remains correct, despite, as we shall see, the fact that those highest "values" underlying the practical interest are and always will be decisively significant in determining the focus of attention of analytical activity (*ordnende Taetigkeit des Denkens*) in the sphere of the cultural sciences. It has been and remains true that a systematically correct scientific proof in the social sciences, if it is to achieve its purpose, must be acknowledged as correct even by a Chinese — or — more precisely stated — it must constantly *strive* to attain this goal, which perhaps may not be completely attainable due to faulty data. Furthermore, the successful *logical* analysis of the content of an ideal and its ultimate axioms and the discovery of the consequences which arise from pursuing it, logically and practically, must also be valid for the Chinese. At the same time, our Chinese can lack a "sense" for our ethical imperative and he can and certainly often will deny the ideal itself and the concrete value-judgments derived from it. Neither of these two latter attitudes can affect the scientific value of the analysis in any way. Quite certainly our journal will not ignore the ever and inevitably recurrent attempts to give an unambiguous interpretation to culture. On the contrary, these attempts themselves rank with the most important products of this cultural life and, under certain circumstances, among its dynamic forces. We will therefore constantly strive to follow with care the course of these discussions of "social philosophy" (as here understood). We are furthermore completely free of the prejudice which asserts that reflections on culture which go beyond the analysis of empirical data in order to interpret the world metaphysically can, because of their metaphysical character fulfil no useful cognitive tasks. Just what these cognitive tasks are is primarily an epistemological question, the answer to which we must and can, in view of our purpose, disregard at this point. There is one tenet to which we adhere most firmly in our work, namely, that a social science journal, in our sense, to the extent that it is *scientific* should be a place where those truths are sought, which—to remain with our illustration—can claim, even for a Chinese, the validity appropriate to an analysis of empirical reality.

Of course, the editors cannot once and for all deny to themselves or their contributors the possibility of expressing in value-judgments the ideals which motivate them. However two important duties arise in connection with this. First, to keep the readers and themselves sharply aware at every moment of the standards by which they judge reality and from which the value-judgment is derived, instead of, as happens too often, deceiving themselves in the conflict of ideals by a value mélange of values of the most different orders and types, and seeking to offer something to everybody. If this obligation is rigorously heeded, the practical evaluative attitude can be not only harmless to scientific interests but even directly useful, and indeed mandatory. In the scientific criticism of legislative and other practical recommendations, the motives of the legislator and the ideals of the critic in all their scope can not be clarified and analyzed in a tangible and intelligible form in any other way than through the confrontation of the standards of value underlying the ideas criticized with others, preferably the critic's own. Every meaningful *value-judgment* about someone else's *aspirations* must be a criticism from the standpoint of one's own *Weltanschauung*; it must be a struggle against *another's* ideals from the standpoint of one's own. If in a particular concrete case, the ultimate value-axioms which underlie practical activity are not only to be designated and scientifically analyzed but are also to be shown in their relationship to *other* value-axioms, "positive" criticism by means of a systematic exposition of the latter is unavoidable.

In the pages of this journal, especially in the discussion of legislation, there will inevitably be found social *policy,* i.e., the statement of ideals, in addition to social *science,* i.e., the analysis of facts. But we do not by any means intend to present such discussions as "science" and we will guard as best we can against allowing these two to be confused with each other. In such discussions, *science* no longer has the floor. For that reason, the second fundamental imperative of scientific freedom is that in such cases it should be constantly made clear to the readers (and — again we say it — above all to one's self!) exactly at which point the scientific investigator becomes silent and the evaluating and acting person begins to speak. In other words, it should be made explicit just where the arguments are addressed to the analytical understanding and where to the sentiments. The constant confusion of the scientific discussion of facts and their evaluation is still one of the most widespread and also one of the most damaging traits of work in our field. The foregoing arguments are directed against this confusion, and not against the clear-cut introduction of one's own ideals into the discussion. An *attitude of moral indifference* has no connection with *scientific* "objectivity." The *Archiv*, at least in its intentions, has never been and should never be a place where polemics against certain currents in politics or social policy are carried on, nor should it be a place where struggles are waged for or against ideals in politics or social-policy. There are other journals for these purposes. The peculiar characteristic of the journal has rather been from the very beginning and, insofar as it is in the power of the editors, shall continue to be that political antagonists can meet in it to carry on scientific work. It has not been a "socialist" organ hitherto and in the future it shall not be "bourgeois." It excludes no one from its circle of contributors who is willing to place himself within the framework of scientific discussion. It cannot be an arena for "objections," replies and rebuttals, but in its pages no one will be protected, neither its contributors nor its editors, from being subjected to the sharpest factual, scientific criticism. Whoever cannot bear this or who takes the viewpoint that he does not wish to work, in the service of

scientific knowledge, with persons whose other ideals are different
from his own, is free not to participate. . . .

* * *

. . . it may be asserted without the possibility of a doubt that
as soon as one seeks to derive concrete directives from practical
political (particularly economic and social-political) evaluations,
(1) the indispensable means, and (2) the inevitable repercussions,
and (3) the thus conditioned competition of numerous possible
evaluations in their *practical* consequences, are all that an *empirical* discipline can demonstrate with the means at its disposal.
Philosophical disciplines can go further and lay bare the "meaning"
of evaluations, i.e., their ultimate meaningful structure and their
meaningful consequences, in other words, they can indicate their
"place" within the totality of all the possible "ultimate" evaluations and delimit their spheres of meaningful validity. Even such
simple questions as the extent to which an end should sanction unavoidable means, or the extent to which undesired repercussions
should be taken into consideration or how conflicts between
several concretely conflicting ends are to be arbitrated, are entirely matters of choice or compromise. There is no (rational or empirical) scientific procedure of any kind whatsoever which can
provide us with a decision here. The social sciences, which are
strictly empirical sciences, are the least fitted to presume to save
the individual the difficulty of making a choice, and they should
therefore not create the impression that they can do so.

Finally it should be explicitly noted that the recognition of
the existence of this situation is, as far as our disciplines are concerned, completely independent of the attitude one takes toward
the very brief remarks made above regarding the theory of value.
For there is, in general, no logically tenable standpoint from
which it could be denied except a hierarchical ordering of values
unequivocally prescribed by *ecclesiastical* dogmas. I need not
consider whether there really are persons who assert that such problems as (*a*) does a concrete event occur thus and so or otherwise,
or (*b*) why do the concrete events in question occur thus and so
and not otherwise, or (*c*) does a given event ordinarily succeed
another one according to a certain law and with what degree of
probability — are not basically different from the problems:
(*a1*) what should one do in a concrete situation, or (*b2*) from which
standpoints may those situations be satisfactory or unsatisfactory,

or (*c3*) whether they are — whatever their form — generally formulatable propositions (axioms) to which these standpoints can be reduced. There are many who insist further that there is no logical disjunction between such inquiries as, (*a*) in which direction will a concrete situation (or generally, a situation of a certain type) develop and with what greater degree of probability in which particular direction than in any other and (*b*) a problem which investigates whether one *should* attempt to influence the development of a certain situation in a given direction — regardless of whether it be the one in which it would also move if left alone, or the opposite direction or one which is different from either. There are those who assert that (*a*) the problem as to which attitudes towards any given problem specified persons or an unspecified number of persons under specified conditions will probably or even certainly take and (*b*) the problem as to whether the attitude which emerged in the situation referred to above is *right* — are in no way different from one another. The proponents of such views will resist any statement to the effect that the problems in the above-cited juxtapositions do not have even the slightest connection with one another and that they really are "to be separated from one another." These persons will insist furthermore that their position is not in contradiction with the requirements of scientific thinking. Such an attitude is by no means the same as that of an author who conceding the absolute heterogeneity of both types of problems, nevertheless, in one and the same book, on one and the same page, indeed in a principal and subordinate clause of one and the same sentence, makes statements bearing on each of the two heterogeneous problems referred to above. Such a procedure is strictly a matter of choice. All that can be demanded of him is that he does not unwittingly (or just to be clever) deceive his readers concerning the absolute heterogeneity of the problems. Personally I am of the opinion that nothing is too "pedantic" if it is useful for the avoidance of confusions.

Thus, the discussion of value-judgments can have only the following functions:

a) The elaboration and explication of the ultimate, internally "consistent" value-axioms, from which the divergent attitudes are derived. People are often in error, not only about their opponent's evaluations, but also about their own. This procedure is essentially an operation which begins with concrete particular evaluations and analyzes their meanings and then moves to the more general level of irreducible evaluations. It does not use the techniques of an empirical discipline and it produces no new knowledge of facts. Its "validity" is similar to that of logic.

b) The deduction of "implications" (for those accepting certain value-judgments) which follow from certain irreducible value-axioms, when the practical evaluation of factual situations is based on these axioms alone. This deduction depends on one hand, on logic, and on the other on empirical observations for the completest possible casuistic analyses of all such empirical situations as are in principle subject to practical evaluation.

c) The determination of the factual consequences which the realization of a certain practical evaluation must have: (1) in consequence of being bound to certain indispensable means, (2) in consequence of the inevitability of certain, not directly desired repercussions. These purely empirical observations may lead us to the conclusion that (a) it is absolutely impossible to realize the object of the preference, even in a remotely approximate way, because no means of carrying it out can be discovered; (b) the more or less considerable improbability of its complete or even approximate realization, either for the same reason or because of the probable appearance of undesired repercussions which might directly or indirectly render the realization undesirable; (c) the necessity of taking into account such means or such repercussions as the proponent of the practical postulate in question did not consider, so that his evaluation of end, means, and repercussions becomes a new problem for him. Finally: (d) the uncovering of new axioms (and the postulates to be drawn from them) which the proponent of a practical postulate did not take into consideration. Since he was unaware of those axioms, he did not formulate an attitude towards them although the execution of his own postulate conflicts with the others either (1) in principle or (2) as a result of the practical consequences, (i.e., logically or actually). In (1) it is a matter in further discussion of problems of type (*a*); in (2), of type (*c*).

Far from being meaningless, value-discussions of this type can be of the greatest utility as long as their potentialities are correctly understood.

The utility of a discussion of practical evaluations at the right place and in the correct sense is, however, by no means exhausted with such direct "results." When correctly conducted, it can be extremely valuable for empirical research in the sense that it provides it with problems for investigation.

The problems of the empirical disciplines are, of course, to be solved "non-evaluatively." They are not problems of evaluation. . . .

6

Values
in Inquiry

Abraham Kaplan

No doubt other generations than our own have felt themselves to be in the grip of "the crisis of our times"; some of them, indeed, were convinced that the world was quite literally coming to an end. It is possible, however, that no other generation has talked about its crisis so much as we have. That values are changing, that they are in conflict, and that they are altogether precarious is now and has been for some time a part of the general consciousness of the age.

THE CONTENTION ABOUT VALUES

What I think might be distinctively our own is not only the extent of this consciousness but also its depth, the fact that its doubts and anxieties are so radical. The term "value" — "that unfortunate child of misery", as Weber has called it—has two sorts of meanings (among many others). It may refer to the standards or principles of worth, what makes something have value, or it may refer to the worthy things themselves, the valuables, as it were (I shall be using

Reprinted by permission of Intext Educational Publishers from Abraham Kaplan, *The Conduct of Inquiry: Methodology for Behavioral Science.* (San Francisco: Chandler Publishing Company, 1964), pp. 370-387. Copyright © 1964 by Chandler Publishing Company. Of the original footnotes, only those for full quotations as opposed to those for phrases have been retained.

the term "value" only in the first sense). Now while valuables have often before been felt to be uncertain, whether in possession or attainment, there has not often been any deep and pervasive doubt as to values, that is, as to whether such things are really valuable, really worth having and pursuing. It is this latter that is now very much in question. There have been various philosophers, like the Greek Sophists and the Carvakas of India, who challenged the basis of the value judgments characteristic of their cultures; but by and large philosophers have been occupied with examining the specific varieties of value, and the conditions, personal or institutional, under which the values can be achieved. In modern times, however, and most notably in contemporary Anglo-American philosophy, there is an almost exclusive preoccupation with the basis of value judgments rather than with their content. We have still some sense of what is true, honorable, just, pure, lovely, or gracious, and we think of these things; but we do not any more really know what we are saying about things when we ascribe to them these excellences.

This condition of the culture has a direct bearing on the situation of the sciences, and especially of behavioral science, which might be expected to be the one most closely concerned with questions of values. Whether in fact or only in the public mind, science is responsible for the value crisis. The technology which it has made possible has produced the great changes that threaten our valuables, and the ways of thinking which it has engendered undermine the very values themselves. There is, therefore, a widespread attitude towards science (or against it, rather) that with regard to values, the policy must be strictly "Hands off!" Science has done enough harm already, and the scientist should be grateful that he is allowed to go on about his business. In thus protecting values *from* science, this attitude gives up the possibility of supporting values *by* science. By limiting reason we may make room for faith, but we have room enough if we have little faith, and who shall supply our lack? Limiting reason is the policy of achieving the security of the value domain by sacrificing freedom— the freedom, that is, to enrich our lives in whatever ways our knowledge and experience show to be open to us.

There is a contrary attitude, often ambivalently associated with the preceding one, that the scientist *must* occupy himself with values. Here it is precisely the attempt by science to abstract the facts from their value matrix which is thought to be most subversive of values. Thus the psychoanalyst is charged with encouraging libertinism because as a theorist his aim and as a therapist his method is to understand the behavior, not to condemn it. Thus an uproar was produced not long ago when a research agency working on a military contract was found to be engaged in a study of surrender situations, as though the study itself compromised the nobility of our old-guard determination to die but not to surrender. Thus studies of the viability of democratic institutions are viewed as their obituaries. Thus countless expressions of similar attitudes can be adduced in connection with inquiries into a variety of matters where important values are at stake, from economic affairs to sexual ones, and beyond—in both directions.

The hands-off policy may express an unconscious fear of the outcome for our values of subjecting them to scientific scrutiny; repression in society may have functions similar to those of the defense mechanism in the individual psyche. It is possible, too, that scientific "objectivity" is felt to be the sin of hubris: Olympian detachment is the prerogative only of the gods. And perhaps it is tacitly (and unreasonably) assumed that to understand everything is to forgive everything. Whatever the causes producing these attitudes, the effect is that from the standpoint of the public the scientist is damned if he takes values into account and is likewise damned if he doesn't.

What I find ironic in this situation is that the scientist himself so often identifies with his aggressors, condemning himself as a scientist if he is concerned with values and as a citizen if he is not. But the distinctive roles can provide refuge only for a quick-change artist: the blows still smart when we have put on a new hat. I venture to say that most scientists today, in the free world at any rate, embrace the ideal of a value-free science: they might apply the term "science" also to certain normative disciplines, but properly speaking they regard only "positive" (that is, nonnormative) science as truly scientific. If the student of politics, for example, sets forth a conception of good government or of good society, what he has produced is a political doctrine, not a contribution to political science, whatever the considerations he advances to support his conception. The values may be introduced more or less subtly; Aristotle does not sketch an ideal republic, as Plato does, yet values are basic to his analysis of natural and perverted or degenerate forms of polity. A true scientist, so it is supposed, regards everything as "natural", and he asks only for the conditions under which politics takes one direction or another.

The thesis I want to defend is that not all value concerns are unscientific, that indeed some of them are called for by the scientific enterprise itself, and that those which run counter to scientific ideals can be brought under control—even by the sciences most deeply implicated in the value process.

BIAS

Let me use the term *bias* for adherence to values of such a kind or in such a way as to interfere with scientific objectivity, and let me use it without prejudging whether scientific objectivity requires that science be absolutely value-free. Then, by definition, bias is methodologically objectionable, but the question is still open whether values play a part in the scientific enterprise only as biases. I shall want to answer this question in the negative, and to insist further that this wish is not a matter merely of my own bias.

Typical instances of bias are provided by historians of wars, where the standpoints of the victor and the vanquished yield very different accounts, beginning even with the name of the conflict ("the War Between the States"). And it is a commonplace that bias is more or less easily identifiable in many studies of political, social, or economic problems. We may describe bias in general as a kind of inverse of the genetic fallacy: a proposition is accepted or rejected, not on the basis of its origin, but on the basis of its outcome. It is believed or not according to whether our values would be better served if it were true than if it were false. Of course, this anticipated outcome is not adduced as a reason for the belief, but it operates as a cause of the believing. Indeed, the process is often and even characteristically unconscious. There have been many earnest and hard-headed inquirers into the phenomena of parapsychology; there is at least a possibility that some of them are receptive to positive findings, in spite of themselves, as it were, because of the bearings of such findings on unconscious anxieties about death or on guilts about our less "spiritual" impulses. . . . Freud argued that rejection of his views is traceable to the very resistance which plays such an important part in psychoanalytic theory. Clearly, there is a danger that such charges of unconscious bias can impede the establishment of a truth or the refutation of a mere fancy; but the charges may be logically defensible nevertheless in both sorts of cases.

All propositions, to be sure, are judged on the basis of their implications, and not just in terms of what they entail but also in terms of what they make more likely. What constitutes bias is that the will to believe is motivated by interests external to the context of inquiry itself. I find it useful to distinguish between the scientist's motives and his purposes: *motives* concern the relation between the scientific activity and the whole stream of conduct of which it is a part; *purposes* relate the activities of inquiry to the particular scientific problem which they are intended to solve . . . . Thus a scientist's motives may include the love of country, or of money, or of glory; his purposes must be specified in terms of the particularities of the problem in which he is engaged: to show that a given phenomenon is subject to certain laws, or that a given explanation can be extended to a certain other class of cases, or the like. Various purposes may serve any motive, and various motives may be involved in the decision to fulfill a particular purpose. Bias might be defined as the intrusion of motives, which are extra-scientific, on the fulfillment of scientific purposes.

A beautiful if somewhat analogical instance is described by Edward Lasker, who played a game of chess against a grandmaster at an exposition, where the board was many yards square and the pieces were appropriately costumed young ladies. In the course of the game Lasker gradually realized that his opponent was most reluctant to exchange queens, a tactical weakness in the play of the game which was later explained by the circumstance that a captured piece left for the day, while the grandmaster was most anxious to enjoy afterwards the company of the white queen. Interests external to the play of the game interfered with an objective assessment of the position on the board, or at least, with the choice of the move such an assessment would indicate. It may be worth adding that motivations can contribute to the fulfillment of purposes as well as to their defeat, as Ernest Jones has elaborated in just this context in his analysis of the great chess player Paul Morphy.

I believe that it is the distinction between motives and purposes which underlies the appeal so often made to the difference between the role of the scientist and the role of the citizen, religionist, father, lover, or whatever. Yet each of these roles may define its own purposes, which are not to be confused with the motives that govern the choice of the role in question. There are right ways and wrong ways to do everything, whatever the reasons we may have for doing it.

Bias, then, is not constituted merely by having motives, that is, by subscribing to values which are somehow involved in the scientific situation. Everything depends on the conduct of the inquiry, on the way in which we arrive at our conclusions. Freedom from bias means having an open mind, not an empty one. At the heart of every bias is a prejudice, that is to say, a prejudgment, a conclusion arrived at prior to the evidence and maintained independently of the evidence. It is true that what serves as evidence is the result of a process of interpretation—facts do *not* speak for themselves; nevertheless, facts must be given a hearing, or the scientific point to the process of interpretation is lost. Describe to someone what appears to be the favorable outcome of an experiment on telepathy; he will say that the proportion of successes or the number of cases was too small to be significant. Ask him to suppose that ten times as many cases were taken, and that the results were ten times as favorable; he will suggest that trickery was involved. Continue with the supposition that this is ruled out by the character and integrity of the subjects as well as the investigators, and he will postulate responses to unconscious cues. And if you say, suppose the conditions of the experiment preclude this effect (the subjects being in widely separated rooms, and so on), he will propound some other possible explanation. But at some point, what he *should* say is, "*If* the inquiry and its results *were* as you hypothetically describe them to be, I would believe in telepathy!" The prejudice is betrayed in the determination to adhere to a certain belief no matter what evidence is brought forward. It is this determination or an approximation to it, and not merely having an interest in one conclusion rather than another, which constitutes bias.

There is no doubt that in the history of science biases of this kind, both more and less blatant, have played a significant role.

Identifications with race, class, or nation have made themselves known not just in arguments over priority of discovery but also in decisions as to which theories are acceptable and even which facts are established—nor is this failing limited to such doctrinaires as the Nazis and the Communists. In behavioral science, the scale of radicalism-conservatism may well be "the master scale of biases", affecting both the problems chosen for treatment and the conclusions drawn about whether and how they are to be solved. And everywhere in the scientific enterprise power structures develop, whose interests may have as much effect on the course of inquiry, or at least on the assessment of its outcome, as is exerted by comparable forces on the workings of other enterprises. The influence of the Academy may be as objectionable in science as it is in art . . . .

Every scientist is committed to resisting bias wherever he encounters it, and if we see that he is keen to detect the mote in his neighbor's eye, let us remember that he in turn is *our* neighbor, and beware of judging him. Fortunately, science does not demand that bias be eliminated but only that our judgment take it into account. It can be treated as we are accustomed to deal with errors of observation: we insulate ourselves from them where we can, and otherwise try to cancel their effects or at any rate to discount them. Bias is discounted as a matter of course, for example, when we read a "news" story of the size of a political rally or demonstration, or when we find certain film critics useful because we invariably detest what they recommend. And bias can also be canceled out, as was done by the arbitrator adjudicating a dispute, who returned part of the bribe given him by one of the litigants because the other side had given him a smaller sum.

I believe that the profound significance for science of freedom of thought and its expression is this, that only thereby can we hope to cancel bias. The power structures in science can be relied on to serve the general welfare of the scientific community only if they are subject to some system, however informal, of checks and balances, so that what is rejected by one journal or professional association may find acceptance in another. Perhaps even more important is what Derek Price has called the "invisible university" of our time, constituted by the personal exchange of ideas among highly mobile scientists. That free competition in the marketplace of ideas will invariably yield up the truth may be as much a myth as the more general belief that such a process is the source of every social good. The conflict between freedom and control is an existential dilemma for science, whatever it may be for society at large. Yet for science, at any rate, it seems to me that reason requires that we push always for freedom, freedom even for the thought which we enlightened ones so clearly see to be mistaken.

The question may now be considered whether values play any part in the scientific enterprise in ways which do not necessarily constitute bias. I believe that they do, and in a number of different ways.

VALUES AS SUBJECT-MATTER

To start with, values occur as subject-matter for scientific investigation. In this capacity they do not in the least make for bias, because what is being inquired into is their existence, not their validity. We ask what values are held by various persons and groups, under what conditions and with what effect, and plainly, no answer that we give in itself commits us to sharing or rejecting those values. To be sure, our answer may be a biased one; but if so, the bias is due to *our* values and not to the values of those whom we have been investigating, even if they coincide. It may be hard to recognize that other people have values different from our own, but for that matter it may be just as hard to recognize that other people have beliefs different from ours. To be sure also, if we find that the values we are studying have certain conditions or consequences we may thereby be induced to change some values of our own, so that the prospect of such a change may subtly affect our findings; but again, this influence may apply equally with respect to subject-matters which are not themselves valuational.

The fundamental point is that a proposition affirming something about values is different from a valuation—unless what is being affirmed is precisely the *value* of those values, that is, their validity or worth. Let me call such affirmations *value judgments*; they constitute a special class of judgments about values, namely, those for which making the judgment expresses the judger's own values. Plainly, not every statement which we make about someone's values says something about our own; the statement may be a "factual" one, as it is called, even if it is about values. The recurrent difficulty here is that it is not always easy to see just what a statement does say in this respect, and even the man making it may be unclear in his own mind. The language of behavioral science is often marked by *normative ambiguity*, allowing for interpretation both as reporting a value and as making a valuation. This ambiguity is obviously present in statements about what is "normal" or "natural", but it may also be present in such less obvious cases as "lawful" or "rational". What is worse, normative ambiguity is only temporarily removed, at best, by changing notations. As Myrdal has warned, "In the degree that the new terms would actually cover the facts we discussed in the old familiar terms—the facts which we want to discuss, because we are interested in them—they would soon become equally value-loaded in a society permeated by the same ideals and interests".[1] Talk about "deviant" behavior, for example, has by now about as much normative ambiguity as the old-fashioned talk about "abnormal" behavior.

There are certain propositions about values that unequivocally appear to be making valuations—they seem unambiguously normative—yet are actually factual in content. Nagel calls them "characterizing value judgments", affirming that "a given characteristic is in some degree present (or absent) in a given instance", and contrasts them with "appraising value judgments", which conclude that "some envisaged or actual state of affairs is worthy of approval or disapproval".[2] Thus, we can say that someone is a "good Nazi" without necessarily meaning thereby that being a Nazi is in any way good; we are saying only that certain characteristics are present in that instance without committing ourselves as to whether they are worthy of approval. That this distinction is not an absolute one will be argued in discussing the ethics of the profession, below. But it can usefully be made relative to any given context. Although appraisals may entail certain characteristics, we can characterize without appraising, Nagel insists; at any rate, we can surely characterize without then and there making appraisals of just those things being characterized. We can judge that something conforms to a certain standard without making *that* standard our own, even though the judgment may presuppose our own standards of what conformity is.

VALUES IN THE ETHICS OF THE PROFESSION

Values occur in a second way in science without making for bias, as constituting the ethics of the profession; here, indeed, they work to eradicate bias, or at least to minimize it and to mitigate its effects. That certain professional pursuits have moral prerequisites is beyond question; I am saying, in the broadest sense of the term "moral", the same of scientific pursuits. In our society it is usually taken for granted that moral prerequisites will be satisfied by those entering politics, medicine, or the church, and that such prerequisites are absent or irrelevant for the army, business, and the law. Science, like the philosophy from which it sprang, has an equivocal status. The love of wisdom or truth is a virtue, yet the first sin was eating of the fruit of the tree of knowledge, and the myth of Faust—that those who seek knowledge sell their souls to the Devil—is thought by many, especially today, to convey a dismal reality.

Yet the expression "a good scientist", as used by scientists themselves, seems to me rather more like "a good man" than like "a good Nazi": it embodies a valuation, conveying an appraisal rather than merely a characterization. Being a scientist in itself commits a man to the values embodied in being a good one. We might say that science is a calling and not an occupation only, or at any rate, that it cannot flourish if it is always an occupation only. And the difference between these two sorts of pursuit lies in this, that we choose an occupation while a calling chooses us; we are impelled to the calling from within, which is to say that we are committed to its values. To be sure, all purposive behavior has its own goals and therefore its own values. But in the case of an occupation the values enter only into the purpose (in the narrow sense introduced earlier), and not also into the motives. The values are operative only in the limited context of the purposive behavior, but the purpose which the behavior is to fulfill may have no intrinsic importance, calling for no emotional investments and not reaching beyond the peripheral regions of the personality.

But the passion for truth is just that—a passion: and the thirst for knowledge may be as insistent and provide as deep satisfactions as do needs less specifically human. To follow his calling, even to do his work, a scientist must have what Aristotle called the "intellectual virtues"; and he must not only have them, but also regard them as virtues, that is, seek and cherish them. In a word, they must be his values.

Thus, the scientific habit of mind is one dominated by the reality principle, by the determination to live in the world as it is and not as we might fantasy it. For the scientist, ignorance is never bliss. A robust sense of reality, in William James's phrase, is above all a willingness to face life with open eyes, whatever may confront our sight. The scientist is humble before the facts, submitting his will to their decision, and accepting their judgment whatever it might be. This humility of his is counterpoised by integrity and honesty, by the courage of his convictions, and—if I may paraphrase—by firmness in the truth as God gives him to see the truth, and not as it is given him by tradition, by the Academy, or by the powers that be. And there is a certain distinctive scientific temper, marked by judiciousness and caution, care and conscientiousness. How far all this view is from the model—or rather, the myth—of science as the work of a disembodied, unfeeling intellect! Surely these attributes of the scientist are all virtues, in the scientist's judgment, as well as in our own; and surely the possession of these virtues is a value to which the scientist has wholeheartedly committed himself.

It is true that what I have described is only an "ideal type", something to which actual scientists only approximate in some degree. But it is nevertheless also an ideal, something to which they aspire. For a man to have a certain value it is not required that he have attained what is in that respect valuable—even the sinner may acknowledge the claims of righteousness. It is also true, as Weber reminds us, that "the belief in the value of scientific truth is the product of certain cultures and is not a product of man's original nature".[3] How and why the scientific mentality arose when it did is an important question. I think myself that a religious attitude—a sense of awe and wonder, and a spirit of dedication—may have played a more positive role than is often recognized. Were there a Scientist's Oath it might well quote from Job: "As long as my breath is in me and the spirit of God is in my nostrils, my lips will not speak falsehood and my tongue will not utter deceit." But whether or not science is in the fullest sense a calling, it has a professional ethics which it seems to me methodology cannot completely ignore.

There is also a *metaprofessional ethics . . .* , a set of values
concerning, not the conduct of inquiry, but the contexts in which
it is carried out. The metaprofessional values consist of the commitments to create and maintain conditions under which science
can exist—for instance, freedom of inquiry, of thought, and of
its expression. Such values are particularly important to the behavioral scientist, for it is he who suffers most from restrictions
on those freedoms. If metaprofessional ethics is a matter of self-
interest, at any rate the self as scientist is the self being served.
But there is no need to be victimized here by our own idealiza-
tions; scientists are as subject to human failings as the rest of us
are. Academic freedom, for instance, is not always matched by
academic responsibility, and scientists may be more concerned
with the priority of discovery than with its significance. Yet these
are admittedly failings. In short, that a scientist has values does
not of itself imply that he is therefore biased; it may mean just
the contrary.

VALUES IN THE SELECTION OF PROBLEMS

Values enter into science, in the third place, as a basis for the selection of problems, the order in which they are dealt with, and the
resources expended on their solution. Weber seems to contrast
"the social sciences" with "the empirical disciplines" in that the
problems of the former "are selected by the value-relevance of the
phenomena treated". But so may be the problems of any kind of
subject-matter. The contrast, if any, is just that behavioral science
deals with matters where the values involved are likely to be more
conspicuous, and perhaps more widely shared, or more directly
affecting many people. Whatever problems a scientist selects, he
selects for a reason, and these reasons can be expected to relate
to his values, or to the values of those who in one way or another
influence his choice.

This obvious point is often obscured, I think by a too facile
distinction between so-called "pure" and "applied" science, as
though values are involved only in the latter. In fact, much of what
is called "applied" science can be seen as such only in a subsequent reconstruction: a theory is developed in the course of dealing with a problem of so-called "application", it is abstracted

from such contexts, then afterwards referred back to them as "applied science". A great deal of science, in other words, is "applied" long before it is "pure". The fact that a scientist has reasons for his choice of problems other than a thirst for knowledge or a love of truth scarcely implies that his inquiry will be biased thereby.

That so much of the research carried on today is subsidized by government and industry does not in itself create new dangers to scientific objectivity: research has always had to be paid for by someone or other. The real dangers, it seems to me, lie in the pressures for too quick a return on investments, and perhaps even more in the scarcity of risk capital, the reluctance to depart too far from what the Academy judges to be sound and promising. Artists have long had their patrons and have not for just that reason created bad art. It may even be doubted whether better art might have been produced if they had created only for other artists, or for critics: bohemia is not the sole habitat of genius and integrity. Values make for bias, not when they dictate problems, but when they prejudge solutions.

VALUES AND MEANINGS

Values also play a part in science, and especially in behavioral science, as determinants of the *meanings* which are seen in the events with which it deals. But here the confusion between act meaning and action meaning is especially dangerous.[4]

Weber, for example, has argued that behavioral science cannot even have a subject-matter except as marked out by certain values: "Knowledge of cultural events is inconceivable except on a basis of the significance which the concrete constellations of reality have for us in certain indvidual concrete situations. In which sense and in which situations this is the case . . . is decided according to the value-ideas in the light of which we view 'culture' in each individual case."[5] Interpretation he then defines as the consideration of the "various possible relationships of the object to values."[6] Very well; but the question is, whose values? Cultural events must have a significance, or they are only biophysical occurrences but in this respect it is not, as he says, the significance which they have for us which matters. It is the significance for the actor (and those interacting with him) which makes an act a determinate action.

Thus, in speaking of mental illness the psychologist is no more dependent on his own values than the pathologist is in speaking of organic illness. It is true that what is a symptom of illness in one culture may not be a symptom of the same condition in another; but it is the culture of the subject which counts here, not the scientist's culture. And the subject's culture counts, not because its values define health and illness, but because they determine the *meaning* of the behavior in question. It is not that what is psychopathic in one culture may not be so in another, but rather that a different "what" is occurring in the two cases. And how "*we* view 'culture' in each individual case" has nothing to do with it. The problem posed by this example is complicated by the normative ambiguity of the terms "health" and "illness", so that a diagnosis may be viewed either as a characterizing judgment or as an appraisal. My point is that before either sort of judgment is made the acts in question must be interpreted, and that for this interpretation our values are not decisive.

With respect to action meaning, however, the situation is quite different. Here it is a matter of the sorts of conceptualizations we will apply, the formulations we will give to the problem, the hypotheses we will entertain and the theories we will invoke. In all these we are making choices, and our values inescapably play a part. Here it is significance for us which is involved, though this involvement does not make our interpretation pejoratively "subjective".

There is an extensive literature examining the influence on science of various interests and institutions. These range from the most general metaphysical concerns, whose effect is discussed, for instance, by Philipp Frank, E. A. Burtt, F. S. C. Northrop, and others, to the most specific sexual interests studied by Freud and his followers. And in between are a number of other interests: religious, as traced by Weber, Tawney, and Robert Merton; social and technological, as examined in the work of Veblen, Lewis Mumford, and countless others; Marxist economic determinants; political interests and institutions, from Nietzsche's will to power to the studies of Karl Popper and M. Polanyi; and even esthetic concerns, whose implications for science have been pointed to by

Bergson, L. L. Whyte, and Herbert Read. To be sure, such factors have also another part to play: they do not necessarily predetermine what inquiry will disclose, but give shape and substance to the interpretation of its results.

What I have in mind might be illustrated by the role of key metaphors in various periods of science, the sorts of models which dominate thinking. The eighteenth century was much given to clockwork conceptions, from theology to economics; the nineteenth century to organismic ideas, from the theory of the state to the application of principles of growth and decay in philology; and the twentieth century, to formulations in terms of the workings of a computer, appearing throughout behavioral science. (These three sorts of models might be said to correspond respectively to the basic categories of matter, energy, and information.) The point is that in most of their application these ways of formulating both problems and solutions are to some degree metaphoric, conceptualizing their subject-matters as though they were something other than what they actually are. But our own metaphors always tend to present themselves to us as literal truths. They are the ways of speaking which make sense to us, not just as being meaningful but as being sensible, significant, to the point. They are basic to semantic explanation and thereby enter into scientific explanation. If there is bias here it consists chiefly in the failure to recognize that other ways of putting things might prove equally effective in carrying inquiry forward. But that we must choose one way or another, and thus give our values a role in the scientific enterprise, surely does not in itself mean that we are methodologically damned.

VALUES AND FACTS

But the judgment whether a particular choice is an effective one is itself in some degree a matter of our values. Whether a particular way of conceptualizing problems yields solutions for them is a question of fact, but values enter into the determination of what constitutes a *fact*. Here is the central issue in the question whether science ought to be, or even can be, value-free. I am not referring to the effect of values on the willingness to embark on an inquiry into a question of fact. Here, indeed, we are likely to encounter bias, as in the refusal of Galileo's colleagues to look through his telescope, or in the difference between British and American attitudes today toward psychic research or investigations of telepathy. ... What is at stake here is the role of values, not in our decisions where to look but in our conclusions as to what we have seen.

Nature might better be spoken of an an obedient child than as a protective mother: she speaks only when spoken to, is often seen but seldom heard. Data come to us only in answer to questions, and it is we who decide not only whether to ask but also how the question is to be put. Every question is a little like the wife-beating one—it has its own presuppositions. It must be formulated in a language with a determinate vocabulary and structure, the contemporary equivalent of Kant's forms and categories of the knowing mind; and it follows upon determinate assumptions and hypotheses, on which the answer is to bear. How we put the question reflects our values on the one hand, and on the other hand helps determine the answer we get. If, as Kant said, the mind is the lawgiver to nature, it also has a share in facts, for these are not independent of the laws in terms of which we interpret and acknowledge their factuality. Data are the product of a process of interpretation, and though there is some sense in which the materials for this process are "given" it is only the product which has a scientific status and function. In a word, data have meaning, and this word "meaning", like its cognates "significance" and "import", includes a reference to values. "The empirical data," says Weber, "are always related to those evaluative ideas which alone make them worth knowing and the significance of the empirical data is derived from these evaluative ideas."[7]

There are behavioral scientists who, in their anxieties about bias, hope to exclude values by eschewing theories altogether, in the spirit (but not in the meaning!) of Newton's "I invent no hypotheses!" They restrict themselves to what they regard as "just describing what objectively happens". But this restriction expresses "the dogma of immaculate perception" all over again. What is thus being attempted simply cannot be done, or if it is done, the outcome is of no scientific significance. There is an interesting parallel here to the position of the esthetes at the turn of the century, who viewed art as a matter of pure form or decoration, at the cost of making of it an idle song for an idle hour, with no significance for anyone but themselves. What is even more basic is that, even if carried out, this program does not succeed in eradicating bias. As Myrdal points out, "Biases in social science cannot be erased simply by 'keeping to the facts' and by refined methods of statistical treatment of the data. Facts, and the handling of data, sometimes show themselves even more pervious to tendencies towards bias than does 'pure thought'."[8] . . .

Nagel has argued that "there is no factual evidence to show that the 'content and form' of statements, or the standards of validity employed, are logically determined by the social perspective of an inquirer. The facts commonly cited establish no more than some kind of causal dependence between thse items."[9] This argument is sound if "logical determination" has the sense of entailment; indeed, no factual evidence can possibly be given for an entailment. But this is not to say that what is "no more than some kind of causal dependence" can have no methodological import. To ignore some of the evidence, for example, is illogical: even though ignoring it does not *entail* that the conclusions arrived at will be false or even improbable, the ignoring may well cause us to arrive at false conclusions. The more basic point, perhaps, is that even though values are not *sufficient* to establish facts it does not follow that they are therefore not *necessary*. The ultimate empiricism on which science rests consists in this, that thinking something is so does not make it so, and this negation applies even more forcibly, if possible, to wishing it were so. The predicted eclipse occurs whether we like it or not, and would have occurred whether it had been predicted or not. But values enter both into making the prediction and into the conceptualization of what "it" is being predicted.[10]

OBJECTIVITY AND VALUES

I believe that the insistence on science as value-free stems from the very proper determination to free science from any imputation of a subjective relativism, of the kind that may well be involved in certain conceptions of the sociology of knowledge and of "class science". But whether conceding that values have an inescapable part to play in the scientific enterprise has this consequence depends on the theory of value which is brought to bear. The objectivity of science demands its being value-free only if values are necessarily and irreducibly subjective. I agree with the proponents of value-free science in this basic respect, that *either* values (as appraisals) must be rigorously excluded from science, or *else* they must themselves be given an objective ground. It is this second alternative which seems to me methodologically sounder. For I do not see how values *can* be excluded. With Myrdal, I believe that "the attempt to eradicate biases by trying to keep out the valuations themselves is a hopeless and misdirected venture. . . . There is no other device for excluding biases in social sciences [or any other] than to face the valuations and to introduce them as explicitly stated, specific, and sufficiently concretized value premises."[11] And, I would add, to provide an objective basis for them. The problem for methodology is not *whether* values are involved in inquiry, but *which,* and above all, how they are to be empirically grounded. . . .

NOTES

1. Gunnar Myrdal, "Methodological Note on Facts and Valuations in Social Science," in his *An American Dilemma* (New York: Harper and Row, 1944), pp. 1063-1064.

2. Ernest Nagel, *The Structure of Science* (New York: Harcourt, Brace and World, 1961), pp. 492-493.

3. Max Weber, *The Methodology of Social Sciences* (New York: Free Press of Glencoe, 1949), p. 10.

4. For Professor Kaplan's discussion of the difference between "act meaning" and "action meaning," see *The Conduct of Inquiry* (San Francisco: Chandler, 1964), pp. 358-359. [Ed.]

5. Weber, *op. cit.,* p. 80.

6. *Ibid.,* p. 143.

7. *Ibid.,* p. 111.

8. Myrdal, *op. cit.,* p. 1041.

9. Ernest Nagel, "Some Issues in the Logic of Historical Analysis," *The Structure of Scientific Thought,* edited by Edward H. Madden (Boston: Houghton Mifflin, 1960), p. 193.

10. For a fuller discussion of this issue, see Kaplan, *op. cit.,* pp. 250-257. [Ed.]

11. Myrdal, *op. cit.,* p. 1043.

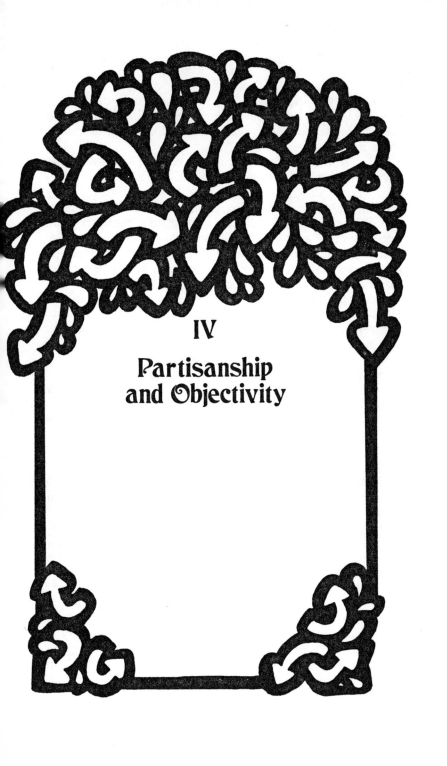

IV

Partisanship
and Objectivity

The two concluding essays, along with the accompanying "replies," raise the issue of an objective social science within the contexts of the sociology of knowledge and a theory about the hierarchical structure of society.

In "Whose Side Are We On?" the sociologist Howard S. Becker is concerned with two questions. First, under what circumstances are sociologists accused, either by themselves or by outsiders, of bias? And second, under what conditions are such accusations true? By dividing situations that sociologists study into "political" and "apolitical" cases and applying a principle that he designates the "hierarchy of credibility," Professor Becker skillfully analyzes in what situations, by whom, and for what reasons sociologists are accused of bias and distortion. His conclusion is that in "apolitical" cases the sociologist is accused of bias when he conducts his research from the standpoint of subordinates—for example, from the point of view of youth, blacks, or criminals. The reason is that the sociologist is perceived to have violated the principle of the "hierarchy or credibility," which states that in any system of ranked groups, superordinates have the right to define the way things really are. In situations where conflict is highly organized ("political" cases), bias is charged regardless of whether the sociologist adopts the standpoint of subordinates or that of superordinates. If he speaks for subordinates, he once again violates the principle of the "hierarchy of credibility." On the other hand, if he takes the side of superordinates, he is thought to be guilty of maintaining the status quo.

Becker's answer to the second question is less clear than his answer to the first one. He seems to believe, however, that in both "apolitical" and "political" cases, accusations of bias are justified. Since society (according to Becker) is structured in hierarchical patterns, the sociologist cannot avoid conducting his research from some point of view. But to conduct research from a point of view is to become the partisan (or biased) spokesman for those who occupy the standpoint in question. Furthermore, neither making improved use of the "tools and techniques" of sociology (questionnaires, interviews, etc.) nor limiting the range of sociological theories will correct matters. Consequently, it appears that Becker believes an objective (in the sense of "unbiased") sociology to be impossible, for "there is no position from which sociological research can be done that is not biased in one or another way."

In my essay "Partisanship and Objectivity in the Social Sciences," I undertake a critical examination of Becker's—and, it should be noted, Gouldner's (1968)—central theme, namely, the necessity for all sociological research to be conducted from partisan or biased points of view. Two lines of argument are developed. First, Becker's conclusion is shown to follow from his analysis of social structure in terms of hierarchically ordered institutions and from his uncritical acceptance of one version of the sociology of knowledge. Against these background assumptions it is argued that, as an epistemological theory, the version of the sociology of knowledge in question is self-referentially inconsistent—that is, any formal statement of the theory will show it either to be false or to be meaningless to opponents of the theory. The second line of argument consists of an analysis of "points of view" and "conducting research from a point of view," phrases that are central to Becker's conclusion. With respect to the first phrase, it is argued that society's being structured hierarchically results in biased sociological research *only if* each stratum among the ranked groups has its own unique values and beliefs. With respect to the second phrase, it is argued that conducting research from a point of view results in bias *only if* the researcher must adopt *all* the values and beliefs that define the point of view. I contend that neither condition holds. The conclusion drawn from the two lines of argument is that Becker has failed to provide convincing reasons for believing either (1) that all sociological research must be conducted from special points of view or (2) that if, *ex hypothesi,* sociological research must be conducted from special points of view, the sociologist is necessarily partisan or biased.

A rejoinder by each author follows the principal essays of this section. In his "Reply" Becker attempts to clarify his position by contending that he does not accept the tenets of the relativistic epistemology I ascribed to him. Objective sociological research, he writes, is not (in principle) an unattainable goal. It is only in the sense of favoring or appearing to favor one side or another in a social controversy that sociologists are inevitably biased. In response I argue that although favoring or appearing to favor a given side in a social controversy may provide grounds for an *accusation* of bias, that is not in itself the same as to *be* biased. As a result, Becker's "clarified" position raises a question as to the claim he is making. Is it that, given the nature of social controversy, sociologists will inevitably be accused of bias? Or is it that sociologists are inevitably biased in a sense other than that of simply favoring one side or another in a controversy? If Becker's claim is the former, there is little room for disagreement because the point is trivially true. However, if his claim is the latter, I argue that Becker is in fact committed to the epistemological relativism that he is so reluctant to accept.

In addition to Becker's and Riley's papers, the reader should examine Alvin Gouldner's sustained criticism of "Whose Side Are We On?" (Gouldner, 1968). On the bearing of the sociology of knowledge on the issue of an objective social science, there is a wealth of material. The following works are especially relevant: Mannheim (1936), Ch. 5; Bottomore (1956); Child (1947); Gluck (1954); Hartung (1952); Hinshaw (1948); and Nagel (1961, Ch. 13.

7

Whose Side Are We On?

Howard Becker

To have values or not to have values: the question is always with us. When sociologists undertake to study problems that have relevance to the world we live in, they find themselves caught in a crossfire. Some urge them not to take sides, to be neutral and do research that is technically correct and value free. Others tell them their work is shallow and useless if it does not express a deep commitment to a value position.

This dilemma, which seems so painful to so many, actually does not exist, for one of its horns is imaginary. For it to exist, one would have to assume, as some apparently do, that it is indeed possible to do research that is uncontaminated by personal and political sympathies. I propose to argue that it is not possible and, therefore, that the question is not whether we should take sides, since we inevitably will, but rather whose side we are on.

I will begin by considering the problem of taking sides as it arises in the study of deviance. An inspection of this case will soon reveal to us features that appear in sociological research of all kinds. In the greatest variety of subject matter

From Howard S. Becker, "Whose Side Are We On?" *Social Problems,* 14 (Winter 1967), pp. 239-247. Copyright © 1967 by The Society for the Study of Social Problems. Reprinted by permission of *Social Problems,* The Society for the Study of Social Problems, and the author.

areas and in work done by all the different methods at our disposal, we cannot avoid taking sides, for reasons firmly based in social structure.

We may sometimes feel that studies of deviance exhibit too great a sympathy with the people studied, a sympathy reflected in the research carried out. This feeling, I suspect, is entertained off and on both by those of us who do such research and by those of us who, our work lying in other areas, only read the results. Will the research, we wonder, be distorted by that sympathy? Will it be of use in the construction of scientific theory or in the application of scientific knowledge to the practical problems of society? Or will the bias introduced by taking sides spoil it for those uses?

We seldom make the feeling explicit. Instead, it appears as a lingering worry for sociological readers, who would like to be sure they can trust what they read, and a troublesome area of self-doubt for those who do the research, who would like to be sure that whatever sympathies they feel are not professionally unseemly and will not, in any case, seriously flaw their work. That the worry affects both readers and researchers indicates that it lies deeper than the superficial differences that divide sociological schools of thought, and that its roots must be sought in characteristics of society that affect us all, whatever our methodological or theoretical persuasion.

If the feeling were made explicit, it would take the form of an accusation that the sympathies of the researcher have biased his work and distorted his findings. Before exploring its structural roots, let us consider what the manifest meaning of the change might be.

It might mean that we have acquired some sympathy with the group we study sufficient to deter us from publishing those of our results which might prove damaging to them. One can imagine a liberal sociologist who set out to disprove some of the common stereotypes held about a minority group. To his dismay, his investigation reveals that some of the stereotypes are unfortunately true. In the interest of justice and liberalism, he might well be tempted, and might even succumb to the temptation to suppress those findings, publishing with scientific candor the other results which confirmed his beliefs.

But this seems not really to be the heart of the charge, because sociologists who study deviance do not typically hide things about the people they study. They are mostly willing to grant that there is something going on that put the deviants in the position they are in, even if they are not willing to grant that it is what the people they studied were originally accused of.

A more likely meaning of the charge, I think, is this. In the course of our work and for who knows what private reasons, we fall into deep sympathy with the people we are studying, so that while the rest of the society views them as unfit in one or another respect for the deference ordinarily accorded a fellow citizen, we believe that they are at least as good as anyone else, more sinned against than sinning. Because of this, we do not give a balanced picture. We focus too much on questions whose answers show that the supposed deviant is morally in the right and the ordinary citizen morally is in the wrong. We neglect to ask those questions whose answers would show that the deviant, after all, has done something pretty rotten and, indeed, pretty much deserves what he gets. In consequence, our overall assessment of the problem being studied is one-sided. What we produce is a whitewash of the deviant and a condemnation, if only by implication, of those respectable citizens who, we think, have made the deviant what he is.

It is to this version that I devote the rest of my remarks. I will look first, however, not at the truth or falsity of the charge, but rather at the circumstances in which it is typically made and felt. The sociology of knowledge cautions us to distinguish between the truth of a statement and an assessment of the circumstances under which that statement is made; though we trace an argument to its source in the interests of the person who made it, we have still not proved it false. Recognizing the point and promising to address it eventually, I shall turn to the typical situations in which the accusation of bias arises.

When do we accuse ourselves and our fellow sociologists of bias? I think an inspection of representative instances would show that the accusation arises, in one important class of cases, when the research gives credence, in any serious way, to the perspective of the subordinate group in some hierarchical relationship. In the case of deviance, the hierarchical relationship is a moral one. The superordinate parties in the relationship are those who represent the forces of approved and official morality; the subordinate parties are those who, it is alleged, have violated that morality.

Though deviance is a typical case, it is by no means the only one. Similar situations, and similar feelings that our work is biased, occur in the study of schools, hospitals, asylums and prisons, in the study of physical as well as mental illness, in the study of both "normal" and delinquent youth. In these situations, the superordinate parties are usually the official and professional authorities in charge of some important institution, while the subordinates are those who make use of the services of that institution. Thus, the police are the superordinates, drug addicts are the subordinates; professors and administrators, principals and teachers, are the superordinates, while students and pupils are the subordinates; physicians are the superordinates, their patients the subordinates.

All of these cases represent one of the typical situations in which researchers accuse themselves and are accused of bias. It is a situation in which, while conflict and tension exist in the hierarchy, the conflict has not become openly political. The conflicting segments or ranks are not organized for conflict; no one attempts to alter the shape of the hierachy. While subordinates may complain about the treatment they receive from those above them, they do not propose to move to a position of equality with them, or to reverse positions in the hierarchy. Thus, no one proposes that addicts should make and enforce laws for policemen, that patients should prescribe for doctors, or that adolescents should give orders to adults. We can call this the *apolitical* case.

In the second case, the accusation of bias is made in a situation that is frankly political. The parties to the hierarchical relationship engage in organized conflict, attempting either to maintain or change existing relations of power and authority. Whereas in the first case subordinates are typically unorganized and thus have, as we shall see, little to fear from a researcher, subordinate parties in a political situation may have much to lose. When the situation is political, the researcher may accuse himself or be accused of bias by someone else when he gives credence to the perspective of either party to the political conflict. I leave the political for later and turn now to the problem of bias in apolitical situations.[1]

We provoke the suspicion that we are biased in favor of the subordinate parties in an apolitical arrangement when we tell the story from their point of view. We may, for instance, investigate their complaints, even though they are subordinates, about the way things are run just as though one ought to give their complaints as much credence as the statements of responsible officials. We provoke the charge when we assume, for the purpose of our research, that subordinates have as much right to be heard as superordinates, that they are as likely to be telling the truth as they see it as superordinates, that what they say about the institution has a right to be investigated and have its truth or falsity established, even though responsible officials assure us that it is unnecessary because the charges are false.

We can use the notion of a *hierarchy of credibility* to understand this phenomenon. In any system of ranked groups, participants take it as given that members of the highest group have the right to define the way things really are. In any organization, no matter what the rest of the organization chart shows, the arrows indicating the flow of information point up, thus demonstrating (at least formally) that those at the top have access to a more complete picture of what is going on than anyone else. Members of lower groups will have incomplete information, and their view of reality will be partial and distorted in consequence. Therefore, from the point of view of a well socialized participant in the system, any tale told by those at the top intrinsically deserves to be regarded as the most credible account obtainable of the organizations' workings. And since, as Summer pointed out, matters of rank and status are contained in the mores,[2] this belief has a moral quality. We are, if we are proper members of the group, morally bound to accept the definition imposed on reality by a superordinate group in preference to the definitions espoused by subordinates. (By analogy, the same argument holds for the social classes of a community.) Thus, credibility and the right to be heard are differentially distributed through the ranks of the system.

As sociologists, we provoke the charge of bias, in ourselves and others, by refusing to give credence and deference to an established status order, in which knowledge of truth and the right to be heard are not equally distributed. "Everyone knows" that re-

sponsible professionals know more about things than laymen, that
police are more respectable and their words ought to be taken
more seriously than those of the deviants and criminals with
whom they deal. By refusing to accept the hierarchy of credibility, we express disrespect for the entire established order.

We compound our sin and further provoke charges of bias
by not giving immediate attention and "equal time" to the apolo-
gies and explanations of official authority. If, for instance, we
are concerned with studying the way of life inmates in a mental
hospital build up for themselves, we will naturally be concerned
with the constraints and conditions created by the actions of the
administrators and physicians who run the hospital. But, unless
we also make the administrators and physicians the object of our
study (a possibility I will consider later), we will not inquire into
why those conditions and constraints are present. We will not
give responsible officials a chance to explain themselves and give
their reasons for acting as they do, a chance to show why the
complaints of inmates are not justified.

It is odd that, when we perceive bias, we usually see it in
these circumstances. It is odd because it is easily ascertained that
a great many more studies are biased in the direction of the interests of responsible officials than the other way around. We may
accuse an occasional student of medical sociology of having given
too much emphasis to the complaints of patients. But is it not
obvious that most medical sociologists look at things from the
point of view of the doctors? A few sociologists may be sufficiently biased in favor of youth to grant credibility to their account of how the adult world treats them. But why do we not
accuse other sociologists who study youth of being biased in favor of adults? Most research on youth, after all, is clearly designed to find out why youth are so troublesome for adults, rather
than asking the equally interesting sociological question: "Why
do adults make so much trouble for youth?" Similarly, we accuse those who take the complaints of mental patients seriously
of bias; what about those sociologists who only take seriously the
complaints of physicians, families and others about mental patients?

Why this disproportion in the direction of accusations of
bias? Why do we more often accuse those who are on the side of

subordinates than those who are on the side of superordinates? Because, when we make the former accusation, we have, like the well socialized members of our society most of us are, accepted the hierarchy of credibility and taken over the accusation made by responsible officials.

The reason responsible officials make the accusation so frequently is precisely because they are responsible. They have been entrusted with the care and operation of one or another of our important institutions: schools, hospitals, law enforcement, or whatever. They are the ones who, by virtue of their official position and the authority that goes with it, are in a position to "do something" when things are not what they should be and, similarly, are the ones who will be held to account if they fail to "do something" or if what they do is, for whatever reason, inadequate.

Because they are responsible in this way, officials usually have to lie. That is a gross way of putting it, but not inaccurate. Officials must lie because things are seldom as they ought to be. For a great variety of reasons, well-known to sociologists, institutions are refractory. They do not perform as society would like them to. Hospitals do not cure people; prisons do not rehabilitate prisoners; schools do not educate students. Since they are supposed to, officials develop ways both of denying the failure of the institution to perform as it should and explaining those failures which cannot be hidden. An account of an institution's operation from the point of view of subordinates therefore casts doubt on the official line and may possibly expose it as a lie.[3]

For reasons that are a mirror image of those of officials, subordinates in an apolitical hierarchical relationship have no reason to complain of the bias of sociological research oriented toward the interests of superordinates. Subordinates typically are not organized in such a fashion as to be responsible for the overall operation of an institution. What happens in a school is credited or debited to the faculty and administrators; they can be identified and held to account. Even though the failure of a school may be the fault of the pupils, they are not so organized that any one of them is responsible for any failure but his own. If he does well, while others all around him flounder, cheat and steal, that is none of his affair, despite the attempt of honor codes to make it so. As long as the sociological report on his school says that every student

there but one is a liar and a cheat, all the students will feel compla-
cent, knowing they are the one exception. More likely, they will
never hear of the report at all or, if they do, will reason that they
will be gone before long, so what difference does it make? The
lack of organization among subordinate members of an institution-
alized relationship means that, having no responsibility for the
group's welfare, they likewise have no complaints if someone ma-
ligns it. The sociologist who favors officialdom will be spared the
accusation of bias.

And thus we see why we accuse ourselves of bias only when
we take the side of the subordinate. It is because, in a situation
that is not openly political, with the major issues defined as
arguable, we join responsible officials and the man in the street
in an unthinking acceptance of the hierarchy of credibility. We
assume with them that the man at the top knows best. We do not
realize that there are sides to be taken and that we are taking one
of them.

The same reasoning allows us to understand why the researcher has the same worry about the effect of his sympathies on his
work as his uninvolved colleague. The hierarchy of credibility is
a feature of society whose existence we cannot deny, even if we
disagree with its injunction to believe the man at the top. When
we acquire sufficient sympathy with subordinates to see things
from their perspective, we know that we are flying in the face of
what "everyone knows." The knowledge gives us pause and causes
us to share, however briefly, the doubt of our colleagues.

When a situation has been defined politically, the second
type of case I want to discuss, matters are quite different. Subordinates have some degree of organization and, with that, spokesmen, their equivalent of responsible officials. Spokesmen, while
they cannot actually be held responsible for what members of
their group do, make assertions on their behalf and are held responsible for the truth of those assertions. The group engages in
political activity designed to change existing hierarchial relationships and the credibility of its spokesmen directly affects its poli-
cal fortunes. Credibility is not the only influence, but the group
can ill-afford having the definition of reality proposed by its
spokesmen discredited, for the immediate consequence will be
some loss of political power.

Superordinate groups have their spokesmen too, and they are confronted with the same problem: to make statements about reality that are politically effective without being easily discredited. The political fortunes of the superordinate group—its ability to hold the status changes demanded by lower groups to a minimum—do not depend as much on credibility, for the group has other kinds of power available as well.

When we do research in a political situation we are in double jeopardy, for the spokesmen of both involved groups will be sensitive to the implications of our work. Since they propose openly conflicting definitions of reality, our statement of our problem is in itself likely to call into question and make problematic, at least for the purposes of our research, one or the other definition. And our results will do the same.

The hierarchy of credibility operates in a different way in the political situation than it does in the apolitical one. In the political situation, it is precisely one of the things at issue. Since the political struggle calls into question the legitimacy of the existing rank system, it necessarily calls into question at the same time the legitimacy of the associated judgements of credibility. Judgements of who has a right to define the nature of reality that are taken for granted in an apolitical situation become matters of argument.

Oddly enough, we are, I think, less likely to accuse ourselves and one another of bias in a political than in an apolitical situation, for at least two reasons. First, because the hierarchy of credibility has been openly called into question, we are aware that there are at least two sides to the story and so do not think it unseemly to investigate the situation from one or another of the contending points of view. We know, for instance, that we must grasp the perspectives of both the residents of Watts and of the Los Angeles policemen if we are to understand what went on in that outbreak.

Second, it is no secret that most sociologists are politically liberal to one degree or another. Our political preferences dictate the side we will be on and, since those preferences are shared by most of our colleagues, few are ready to throw the first stone or are even aware that stone-throwing is a possibility. We usually take the side of the underdog; we are for Negroes and against Fascists. We do not think anyone biased who does research designed to prove that the former are not as bad as people think or

that the latter are worse. In fact, in these circumstances we are
quite willing to regard the question of bias as a matter to be dealt
with by the use of technical safeguards.

We are thus apt to take sides with equal innocence and lack
of thought, though for different reasons, in both apolitical and
political situations. In the first, we adopt the commonsense view
which awards unquestioned credibility to the responsible official.
(This is not to deny that a few of us, because something in our
experience has alerted them to the possibility, may question the
conventional hierarchy of credibility in the special area of our ex-
pertise.) In the second case, we take our politics so for granted
that it supplants convention in dictating whose side we will be on.
(I do not deny, either, that some few sociologists may deviate politically from their liberal colleagues, either to the right or the left,
and thus be more liable to question that convention.)

In any event, even if our colleagues do not accuse us of bias
in research in a political situation, the interested parties will.
Whether they are foreign politicians who object to studies of how
the stability of their government may be maintained in the interest of the United States (as in the *Camelot* affair)[4] or domestic
civil rights leaders who object to an analysis of race problems that
centers on the alleged deficiencies of the Negro family (as in the
reception given to the Moynihan Report),[5] interested parties are
quick to make accusations of bias and distortion. They base the
accusation not on failures of technique or method, but on conceptual defects. They accuse the sociologist not of getting false
data but of not getting all the data relevant to the problem. They
accuse him, in other words, of seeing things from the perspective
of only one party to the conflict. But the accusation is likely to
be made by interested parties and not by sociologists themselves.

What I have said so far is all sociology of knowledge, suggesting by whom, in what situations and for what reasons sociologists
will be accused of bias and distortion. I have not yet addressed the
question of the truth of the accusations, of whether our findings
are distorted by our sympathy for those we study. I have implied
a partial answer, namely, that there is no position from which sociological research can be done that is not biased in one or another way.

We must always look at the matter from someone's point of
view. The scientist who proposes to understand society must, as

Mead long ago pointed out, get into the situation enough to have
a perspective on it. And it is likely that his perspective will be
greatly affected by whatever positions are taken by any or all of
the other participants in that varied situation. Even if his partici-
pation is limited to reading in the field, he will necessarily read
the arguments of partisans of one or another side to a relationship
and will thus be affected, at least, by having suggested to him
what the relevant arguments and issues are. A student of medical
sociology may decide that he will take neither the perspective of
the patient nor the perspective of the physician, but he will necessarily take a perspective that impinges on the many questions that
arise between physicians and patients; no matter what perspective
he takes, his work either will take into account the attitude of
subordinates, or it will not. If he fails to consider the questions
they raise, he will be working on the side of the officials. If he
does raise those questions seriously and does find, as he may,
that there is some merit in them, he will then expose himself to
the outrage of the officials and of all those sociologists who award
them the top spot in the hierarchy of credibility. Almost all the
topics that sociologists study, at least those that have some relation to the real world around us, are seen by society as morality
plays and we shall find ourselves, willy-nilly, taking part in those
plays on one side or the other.

There is another possibility. We may, in some cases, take the
point of view of some third party not directly implicated in the
hierarchy we are investigating. Thus, a Marxist might feel that it
is not worth distinguishing between Democrats and Republicans,
or between big business and big labor, in each case both groups
being equally inimical to the interests of the workers. This would
indeed make us neutral with respect to the two groups at hand,
but would only mean that we had enlarged the scope of the political conflict to include a party not ordinarily brought in whose
view the sociologist was taking.

We can never avoid taking sides. So we are left with the
question of whether taking sides means that some distortion is introduced into our work so great as to make it useless. Or, less
drastically, whether some distortion is introduced that must be
taken into account before the results of our work can be used. I
do not refer here to feeling that the picture given by the research

is not "balanced," the indignation aroused by having a conventionally discredited definition of reality given priority or equality with what "everyone knows," for it is clear that we cannot avoid that. That is the problem of officials, spokesmen and interested parties, not ours. Our problem is to make sure that, whatever point of view we take, our research meets the standards of good scientific work, that our unavoidable sympathies do not render our results invalid.

We might distort our findings, because of our sympathy with one of the parties in the relationship we are studying, by misusing the tools and techniques of our discipline. We might introduce loaded questions into a questionnaire, or act in some way in a field situation such that people would be constrained to tell us only the kind of thing we are already in sympathy with. All of our research techniques are hedged about with precautionary measures designed to guard against these errors. Similarly, though more abstractly, every one of our theories presumably contains a set of directives which exhaustively covers the field we are to study, specifying all the things we are to look at and take into account in our research. By using our theories and techniques impartially, we ought to be able to study all the things that need to be studied in such a way as to get all the facts we require, even though some of the questions that will be raised and some of the facts that will be produced run counter to our biases.

But the question may be precisely this. Given all our techniques of theoretical and technical control, how can we be sure that we will apply them impartially and across the board as they need to be applied? Our textbooks in methodology are no help here. They tell us how to guard against error, but they do not tell us how to make sure that we will use all the safeguards available to us. We can, for a start, try to avoid sentimentality. We are sentimental when we refuse, for whatever reason, to investigate some matter that should properly be regarded as problematic. We are sentimental, especially, when our reason is that we would prefer not to know what is going on, if to know would be to violate some sympathy whose existence we may not even be aware of. Whatever side we are on, we must use our techniques impartially enough that a belief to which we are especially sympathetic could be proved untrue. We must always inspect our work carefully enough to know whether our techniques and theories are open enough to allow that possibility.

Let us consider, finally, what might seem a simple solution to the problems posed. If the difficulty is that we gain sympathy with underdogs by studying them, is it not also true that the super-ordinates in a hierarchical relationship usually have their own superordinates with whom they must contend? Is it not true that we might study those superordinates or subordinates, presenting their point of view on their relations with their superiors and thus gaining a deeper sympathy with them and avoiding the bias of one-sided identification with those below them? This is appealing, but deceptively so. For it only means that we will get into the same trouble with a new set of officials.

It is true, for instance, that the administrators of a prison are not free to do as they wish, not free to be responsive to the desires of inmates, for instance. If one talks to such an official, he will commonly tell us, in private, that of course the subordinates in the relationship have some right on their side, but they fail to under-stand that his desire to do better is frustrated by his superiors or by the regulations they have established. Thus, if a prison admin-istrator is angered because we take the complaints of his inmates seriously, we may feel that we can get around that and get a more balanced picture by interviewing him and his associates. If we do, we may then write a report which *his* superiors will respond to with cries of "bias." They, in their turn, will say that we have not presented a balanced picture, because we have not looked at *their* side of it. And we may worry that what they say is true.

The point is obvious. By pursuing this seemingly simple solu-tion, we arrive at a problem of infinite regress. For everyone has someone standing above him who prevents him from doing things just as he likes. If we question the superiors of the prison adminis-trator, a state department of corrections or prisons, they will com-plain of the governor and the legislature. If we ask the governor and the legislature, they will complain of lobbyists, party machines, the public and the newspapers. There is no end to it and we can never have a "balanced picture" until we have studied all of society simul-taneously. I do not propose to hold my breath until that happy day.

We can, I think, satisfy the demands of our science by always making clear the limits of what we have studied, marking the boundaries beyond which our findings cannot be safely applied. Not just the conventional disclaimer, in which we warn that we have only studied a prison in New York or California and the findings may not hold in the other forty-nine states—which is not a useful procedure anyway, since the findings may very well hold if the conditions are the same elsewhere. I refer to a more sociological disclaimer in which we say, for instance, that we have studied the prison through the eyes of the inmates and not through the eyes of the guards or other involved parties. We warn people, thus, that our study tells us only how things look from that vantage point—what kinds of objects guards are in the prisoners' world—and does not attempt to explain why guards do what they do or to absolve the guards of what may seem, from the prisoners' side, morally unacceptable behavior. This will not protect us from accusations of bias, however, for the guards will still be outraged by the unbalanced picture. If we implicitly accept the conventional hierarchy of credibility, we will feel the sting in that accusation.

It is something of a solution to say that over the years each "one-sided" study will provoke further studies that gradually enlarge our grasp of all the relevant facets of an institution's operation. But that is a long-term solution, and not much help to the individual researcher who has to contend with the anger of officials who feel he has done them wrong, the criticism of those of his colleagues who think he is presenting a one-sided view, and his own worries.

What do we do in the meantime? I suppose the answers are more or less obvious. We take sides as our personal and political commitments dictate, use our theoretical and technical resources to avoid the distortions they might introduce into our work, limit our conclusions carefully, recognize the hierarchy of credibility for what it is, and field as best we can the accusations and doubts that will surely be our fate.

NOTES

1. No situation is necessarily political or apolitical. An apolitcal situation can be transformed into a political one by the open rebel-

lion of subordinate ranks, and a political situation can subside into one in which an accommodation has been reached and a new hierarchy been accepted by the participants. The categories, while analytically useful, do not represent a fixed division existing in real life.

2. William Graham Sumner, "Status in the Folkways," *Folkways* (New York: New American Library, 1960), pp. 72-73.

3. I have stated a portion of this argument more briefly in "Problems of Publication of Field Studies," in Arthur Vidich, Joseph Bensman, and Maurice Stein (eds.), *Reflections on Community Studies* (New York: Wiley, 1964), pp. 267-284.

4. See Irving Louis Horowitz, "The Life and Death of Project Camelot," *Transaction* 3 (Nov./Dec. 1965), pp. 3-7, 44-47.

5. See Lee Rainwater and William L. Yancey, "Black Families and the White House," *ibid.* 3 (July/August 1966), pp. 6-11, 48-53.

8

Partisanship
and Objectivity
in the Social Sciences

Gresham Riley

Two recent and widely discussed essays by sociologists have once
again raised questions concerning the relationship between value
commitments and social inquiry. Is an objective science of social
institutions possible? Can a sociologist, a historian, a political
scientist isolate his moral values or his political sympathies from
his professional investigations? If not, what are the consequences
for the accuracy of his judgments and the adequacy of his explanations and theories? These and other closely related questions are
resurrected by Howard S. Becker's 1966 presidential address to
the Society for the Study of Social Problems and by Alvin W.
Gouldner's caustic, and at times brilliant, response to Becker.[1]
Although Becker and Gouldner explore the role of value commitment solely in the context of sociology, it is clear (as will be evident subsequently) that their views have important implications
for the social sciences in general. Because of these implications
and because of the representative character of Becker's and
Gouldner's conclusions within the larger social scientific community, a careful examination of their position is in order.[2]

    The fact that Becker and Gouldner give expression to the
sentiments of an increasingly large number of social scientists requires that what follows be understood in its proper perspective.

Reprinted by permission from *The American Sociologist*, 6 (February 1971),
pp. 6-12. Copyright © 1971 by The American Sociological Association.

Professionally, I am a student of philosophy, not of the social or behavioral sciences. Consequently, I cannot draw upon a background of research activity to support my observations. The absence of such experience in conjunction with the selection of essays by two prominent sociologists means that my comments will be, in part, those of an "outsider." To persons familiar with contemporary discussions in the philosophy of science, however, it should be evident that philosophers, no less than sociologists, are legitimately concerned with problems related to objectivity and bias in the social sciences.

Becker's and Gouldner's versions of the relationship between value commitment and social inquiry are strikingly similar to Max Weber's well-known dictum: "there is no absolutely 'objective' scientific analysis of culture . . . or of 'social phenomena' independent of special and 'one-sided' viewpoints according to which . . . they are selected, analyzed and organized for expository purpose."[3] Becker states his case as follows:

> There is no position from which sociological research can be done that is not biased in one or another way. . . . We must always look at the matter from someone's point of view. The scientist who proposes to understand society must . . . get into the situation enough to have a perspective on it.[4]

Gouldner repeats the theme. He speaks of the "inevitability of bias" and the "unavoidability of partisanship"; he contends that bias is "inherent in the human condition [and] in sociological research"; and he concludes that "all standpoints are partisan" and that "no one escapes a partisan standpoint."[5]

Holding, as they do, this general conception of social inquiry, Becker and Gouldner deny that sociologists (and, by implication, social scientists in general) should even attempt to formulate explanations or theories that are free of the feelings, wishes, or values of the investigator. For them, the idea of a value-free and unbiased social science is a "myth." For Becker, neutrality with respect to the content of explanations and theories is not even a meaningful, regulative principle. According to him, in order for the latter to be the case, "one would have to assume, as some apparently do, that it is indeed possible to do research that is uncontaminated by personal and political sympathies." He thinks that this is impossible and concludes that the "question is not whether we [sociologists] should take sides, since we inevitably will, but rather whose side are we on."[6]

Rather than develop parallel accounts of the rationale for the above conclusions, I shall concentrate on Becker's "justifications." I do this for two reasons: (1) in terms of the basic claim I am examining—the necessity for all social scientific research to be conducted from "biased points of view"—Gouldner is in essential agreement with Becker and (2) Gouldner is more concerned with the reasons Becker failed to state explicitly whose side he is on and the implications of this failure than he is with providing a defense for the claim that sociologists must inevitably take sides. In contrast, I am interested exclusively in this latter claim.[7]

Why does Becker think that the sociologist must take sides in his professional investigations? And what is the connection he sees between taking sides and getting biased explanations? Answers to these questions should cast additional light on Becker's central thesis and show where he has gone wrong in his analysis.

A possible answer to the first question—why must sociologists take sides in their investigations?—lies in the belief of some sociologists that if their work is to be "relevant" to the problems of the "real world" they must abandon the myth of a value-free science. Taking his cue from the magical word in contemporary educational circles, "relevance," Becker suggests that sociological studies that attempt to be "technically correct and value free" are shallow and useless. Research becomes profound and functional only if the sociologist expresses in his work a "deep commitment to a value position." Overlooking the vagueness of the key concepts in this answer, I understand Becker to be suggesting something like the following: a study on the structure of the Negro family (such as the 1965 Moynihan report) can contribute to resolving race problems only if it reflects a merger of the social scientist's value commitments with, for example, those of his Negro subjects. In other words, if the sociologist is concerned about the social utility of his research, he must take sides.

Such an answer, unfortunately, is too weak for Becker's purposes. A sociologist, it is claimed, does not take sides conditionally; he does so categorically. It is not the case that he becomes a partisan only when he wants his research to be accepted as public policy; he is inevitably a partisan. As Becker observes:

Almost all the topics that sociologists study, at least those
that have some relation to the real world around us, are seen
by society as morality plays and we shall find ourselves, willy-
nilly, taking part in those plays on one side or the other.[8]

What, then, is the source of the unconditional character of
the sociologist's partisanship? For Becker the source is the very
structure of society. "We cannot avoid taking sides," he asserts,
"for reasons firmly based in social structure."[9] Indeed, the fear
of bias associated with taking sides has *its* roots "in characteristics
of society that affect us all, whatever our methodological or theoretical persuasion." The two questions with which we started now
become one question: what is the structure of society that forces
the sociologist to take sides and introduces bias into his research?

The answer is simple. Becker sees society as an array of institutions all of which are structured internally and some of which
are related to each other, in hierarchical patterns. Such patterns
are most evident in and can most clearly be illustrated by institutions concerned with deviant behavior—the kind of behavior that
interests Becker professionally. In a prison system, therefore, the
"chain of being" (to use A. O. Lovejoy's phrase) would be something like the following: prisoners in solitary confinement are at
the bottom; moving upward we find regular inmates, trusties,
guards, the warden, administrators of the state department of cor-
rection, legislators of relevant committees, the governor, lobbyists,
and the electorate. Prisons, too, fit into a ranked system of institutions: the state department of prisons, legislative committees,
the state legislature, lobby groups, the governor's office, etc.

Although society's hierarchical structure is seen most clearly
in institutions concerned with deviance, it is not limited to such
institutions. A similar structure exists in schools, corporations,
and hospitals as well as in the relationship between parents and
children or, at another level, the relationship between youths and
adults. In short, society as seen by Becker is a vast "pecking order"
of superordinates and subordinates, of overdogs and underdogs.

Not only is society characterized by this hierarchical structure,
the structure is sustained by an internal principle of legitimacy.
Becker calls this principle "a hierarchy of credibility." Briefly
stated, the hierarchy of credibility is the belief, taken for granted

in any system of ranked groups, that the superordinates have the right to declare what is real and what is true. They alone are thought to have a coherent picture of the system's various parts. Subordinates, in contrast, are presumed to possess incomplete information; they are said to be unaware of the multiple connections that make up the whole. Consequently, their view of reality and truth is necessarily partial and distorted. Since matters of rank and status are contained in a society's mores, the hierarchy of credibility comes to possess moral force. To be a proper member of society is to be bound morally to accept the definitions of truth and reality given by the superordinates in preference to the definitions of the subordinates. "Credibility and the right to be heard," Becker argues, "are differentially distributed through the ranks of [a] system."[10]

The suggestion is that since society is made up of points of view hierarchically structured, the only foothold a sociologist can get in a study of society is from a particular group's point of view, and no matter what point of view he adopts, the sociologist is subject to bias. If he adopts the point of view of a subordinate, he deviates from "official truth" as defined by the hierarchy of credibility. If he adopts the point of view of a superordinate, he will be biased against subordinate groups who view the hierarchy of credibility as an arbitrary, self-serving principle for maintaining the status quo.

These, then, are the characteristics of social structure which, according to Becker, result in sociologists' inevitably conducting their research from partisan points of view. Clearly this answer is unsatisfactory. Even if we accept Becker's analysis of society's structure, we may legitimately ask: why *must* a sociologist be a partisan? Wherein lies the necessity? Obviously, the structures of society have not prevented Becker from making sociological claims that have the earmarks of objectivity in the usual sense of that word. Consider, for example, that wonderful piece of sociological prose: "credibility and the right to be heard are differentially distributed through the ranks of [a] system." Whose truth is this claim; from whose perspective has it been made? Is it part of the reality of superordinates or subordinates? Becker thinks of it as the reality of neither, for at one point he speaks of the hierarchy of credibility as a principle "everyone knows."[11] But if its truth is known by everyone, it must be true independent of any particular point of view. The characteristics of social structure alone, therefore, do not in themselves inevitably transform scientists into partisans.

To make his claim about sociologists' inevitably taking sides, Becker needs more than a theory about the structure of society; he needs an epistemology. He in fact has one, although it is never more than indirectly disclosed.[12] In particular, he presupposes an epistemological theory that is widely held in sociological circles— the sociology of knowledge.

Influenced by the Marxian notion of ideology, the sociology of knowledge affirms that the concepts in terms of which experience is organized and, in turn, "known" and the canons of truth and validity are socially and historically relative. There can be no analysis of social phenomena that is not an expression of some special social standpoint or that does not reflect the interests and values of some social unit at a given time in history. As Karl Mannheim, a leading exponent of this theory, puts the matter:

> Every epoch has its fundamentally new approach and its characteristic point of view, and consequently sees the "same" objects from a new perspective. . . . The very principles, in the light of which knowledge is to be criticized, are themselves found to be socially and historically conditioned. Hence, their application appears to be limited to given historical periods and the particular types of knowledge then prevalent.[13]

According to the sociology of knowledge, therefore, there can be no objective truth claims concerning society and its institutions. There can be only beliefs that are systematically biased by some social perspective or another, biased by the parochial interests and values of that perspective.

Becker's uncritical employment of the sociology of knowledge and his analysis of social structure permit him to conclude that the sociologist must always investigate from a biased point of view. The sociologist must choose a point of view because society is structured hierarchically, both *in terms of* its institutions and *within* its institutions, and because all knowledge is merely belief conditioned by social perspective. In choosing a point of view, however, the sociologist is inevitably biased, because to take sides is to embrace the definitions of reality and truth of one side against the reality and truth of other standpoints.

Becker's position, then is: (1) all sociological research must be conducted from some point of view, (2) all points of view are biased, and (3) it follows from (1) and (2) that there can be no objective sociological study. That Professor Becker is mistaken is suggested by the fact that his conclusion leads to a reductio ad absurdum. In particular, if Becker is correct, man in society cannot be a proper object for *rational* investigation. This point requires clarification.

Gouldner points out in his response to Becker that "we should try to notice, when men complain about the bonds that enchain them, whether their tone is one of disappointed resent-ment or of comfortable accommodation."[14] It is clear that Becker's tone is one of "comfortable accommodation." Far from being disturbed by his conclusions, Becker proclaims them confi-dently. After all, to ask the question "Whose side are we on?" is to have accepted partisanship as the role of the sociologist.

Faced with Professor Becker's conclusions, I cannot share his equanimity. He has sacrificed too much in his quest for "rele-vance." In denying that there can be objective sociological research Becker is contending that the sociologist can neither know nor use data that do not lend support to the value commitments of "his side." Such data could be utilized only by "changing sides"; but then they would no longer be counterevidence. They would be evidence that supports the value commitments of the newly adopted point of view. Inability to know or use "hostile" data is, however, no small loss for the sociologist. What is at issue is not merely the possibility for objective research but the conditions necessary for any discipline's being a *rational* discipline.

What is a rational discipline? For obvious reasons a complete answer cannot be presented here. A necessary feature, however, is that the discipline's conclusions must be stated in such a way as to make clear what evidence would count against them, and that these conclusions must be open to criticism and even to refutation by critics who successfully marshall such evidence. In denying objectivity (in the above sense) to sociology, Becker has foreclosed on sociology's functioning as a rational discipline.

Once Becker's conclusion is formulated in this manner, the suspicion arises that something has gone wrong with his analysis.

Indeed, the suspicion increases when it is recognized that no rational inquiry of *any* sort into social phenomena is possible. If society is indeed structured as Becker says it is and if all knowledge is belief biased by some standpoint, any discipline that undertakes a study of the institutions of society suffers the same liabilities as sociology. Not only the sociologist but the political scientist, the historian, the anthropologist, the psychologist, and the economist are all partisans who merely plead (nonrationally) the cause of their particular side. Consequently, in evaluating Professor Becker's attack upon objectivity in sociology we can assume that he is in fact denying objectivity to all the social sciences.

The sources of error in Becker's account are: (1) the uncritical use of an indefensible theory of knowledge that Becker himself does not in fact accept and (2) his exploitation of the vagueness of such key phrases as "points of view" and "taking sides." I shall deal with each of these.

As to the uncritical use of an indefensible theory of knowledge, I have noted previously the necessity of Becker's presupposing the sociology of knowledge as an epistemological theory if he is to argue that the social scientist inevitably adopts partisan points of view. It should be evident that the conclusions arrived at by Becker can be maintained only if the sociology of knowledge is understood as asserting a universal and necessary, as opposed to a particular and contingent, relationship between the social perspective and the judgments, explanations, and theories of an inquirer. If it is merely contingently true that a social scientist's pronouncements are colored by the interests and values of some point of view, it should be possible to determine the conditions and circumstances that result in partisanship. But to know the contingent, causal factors of partisanship is to possess the kind of information that enables one to avoid the distorting effect of parochial interests and values. The *inevitability* of adopting biased standpoints is undercut if the sociology of knowledge is just contingently true.

Only the stronger thesis, the thesis that a social perspective enters *necessarily* into the content as well as into the assessment of social scientific theories, can yield Becker's conclusions. This being true, however, Becker's analysis is open to a well-known dialectical difficulty. What, we may legitimately ask, is the cognitive status of the thesis in question? Is it a judgment that simply reflects the values of some point of view—for example the point of view of those who prefer to think of social scientists as partisans? If so, the claim need not be taken seriously by students of the social sciences who hold different perspectives. Indeed, according to the theory itself, it is a claim that cannot be understood by those of us who do not adopt the standpoint of the sociologist of knowledge. In not adopting his standpoint and not finding his thesis meaningful, we are under no constraint to acknowledge the validity of the limitations he would impose upon inquiry.

Or is the thesis for some reason not subject to the controlling influence of perspective that it prescribes to all other assertions? Are its truth and meaning independent of the point of view of those who hold the thesis, independent in the sense that the rest of us who have different social values can understand the claim and evaluate its adequacy? If so, it is not clear why this one thesis is singularly exempt from its own prescription. But, and this is the crucial consideration, if the thesis in question is exempt, it must be a conclusion about the limitations of man's knowledge that is *objective* in the commonsense meaning of this term—that is, in the sense of true, independent of standpoint. If this explanation of the cognitive status of the original thesis is accepted, however, an exception has been made to the theory. And if an exception is to be made in this case, why not in others? Why should the claims that make up the sociology of knowledge be the only ones allowed to be objective? There would appear to be no reason to deny objectivity to an anthropologist's study of primitive religious practices or to a political scientist's analysis of presidential styles if it is to be extended to the study of ideology.

In short, Becker faces the following dilemma: either the epistemological theory that he presupposes in coming to his conclusions is an expression of a particular standpoint or it is an exemption from its own prescriptions. If the former, the theory can have no claim upon those of us who do not share Becker's value commitments; if the latter, the theory is self-referentially inconsistent. In either case, the conclusion that all social scientific research is inevitably conducted from some point of view is left without supporting evidence.[15]

Not only is it the case that the theory of knowledge that underlies Becker's conclusions is indefensible, Becker himself does not in fact subscribe to that theory. There are two examples of his belief that at least some objective claims of knowledge are possible. The first example—Becker's characterization of the "hierarchy of credibility" as a principle known by "everyone"—has already received comment. One can only wonder, if such a principle is available to the sociology of organization structure, why similar principles are not equally available to the sociology of deviant behavior, say, or indeed to all of the social sciences.

The second indication that Becker does not in fact subscribe to the thesis that a social perspective enters necessarily into both the content and the assessment of social scientific theories comes early in his essay where he acknowledges that one can "distinguish between the truth of a statement and an assessment of the circumstances under which that statement is made." To be even more precise, Becker states that "though we trace an argument to its source in the interests of the person who made it, we have still not proved it false"—or true, one might add.[16] I find this a surprising acknowledgment from one who ostensibly holds the above thesis. It is surprising because the sociology of knowledge implies that the categories in terms of which we classify and, in turn, come to know social phenomena and the principles in terms of which we assess the truth of such classifications are socially and historically conditioned. In other words, the advocates of the sociology of knowledge *deny* that the genesis of a proposition is irrelevant to its truth. The passage referred to earlier from Karl Mannheim's *Ideology and Utopia* clearly reflects this stance.

In distinguishing between the truth of a proposition and the circumstances under which it is made Professor Becker seems to be saying, contrary to sociologists of knowledge, that the genesis of a proposition *is irrelevant* to its truth. If this is a fair interpretation of Becker's position, it would appear that he has separated himself from the epistemological tradition which he needs if his conclusions regarding sociological research are to be taken seriously. And it is well that he separates himself from that tradition. For to *deny* that the genesis of a proposition is irrelevant to its truth is to *imply* that once its genesis is known, the question "Is the proposition true?" is no longer an open question. Surely this is not the case. If I am told by Brown that William Rogers is President Nixon's Secretary of State and if subsequently I learn of Brown's moral values, political sympathies, canons of validity, and the characteristic classification schemes of his culture, the question "But is William Rogers the Secretary of State?" is still an open one. The fact that he is is not implied by any of the above circumstances under which Brown might have made the statement. Similarly, to be told by Becker that credibility and the right to be heard are differentially distributed through the ranks of a system is to hear a proposition the truth of which can only be ascertained by examining the way in which social institutions in fact function. No matter how well informed I may be regarding the circumstances under which Becker asserts the proposition, it remains an open question whether credibility and the right to be heard are distributed in the manner described.

My argument is that there are compelling reasons to believe that even Professor Becker does not accept basic tenets of the sociology of knowledge, the very tenets which must be presupposed if he is to argue that sociological research is inevitably conducted from points of view. The point is not that he should be in agreement with the sociology of knowledge but that if he had been clearer about his differences with that tradition, he would not have come to the conclusions he reached about the inevitable partisanship of sociology. Be that as it may, the indefensible character of the sociology of knowledge as an epistemological theory is sufficient to discredit that conclusion.[17]

A second source of error in Becker's analysis is his failure to define precisely such key concepts as "points of view" and "taking sides." Wittgenstein's contention that psychology has experimental methods but conceptual confusions is suggestive at this point.[18] All that is needed is the substitution of "sociology" for "psychology" in the charge. The observation of Wittgenstein is suggestive because Becker's conclusion that sociology cannot excape the bias associated with taking sides is grounded in rather elementary conceptual confusions. Two examples will illustrate this.

First, it is essential to Becker's analysis not only that society be structured in well-defined strata but that each stratum have its unique perspective, its unique value commitments. Otherwise it would not make sense to say that sociological research is always biased because the sociologist, in taking sides, inevitably embraces the definitions of reality and truth of the side taken to the exclusion of all other standpoints. But is it the case that every underdog or subordinate group, for example, possesses a unique perspective? If we take seriously a study such as Bettelheim's "Individual and Mass Behavior in Extreme Situations," the answer is no!

Central to Bettelheim's study of prisoner behavior in German concentration camps is the conclusion that after a period of adjustment the prisoners in these camps tended to adopt the values of the Gestapo. As a subordinate group, the prisoners did *not* possess a unique perspective, they did not possess unique value commitments. The extent of the coalescence of subordinate group values with superordinate group values is carefully noted by Bettelheim. In addition to employing the vocabulary of the Gestapo to express their verbal aggressions, prisoners copied Gestapo techniques of bodily aggression in their treatment of fellow prisoners. To the extent that it was possible, the prisoners styled their uniforms after Gestapo uniforms, they engaged in similar types of leisure-time activity, and they accepted as true (in the absence of indoctrination) Gestapo views on matters of race and politics. In summarizing the role of the concentration camps, Bettelheim states:

> [The concentration camp] is the Gestapo's laboratory where it develops methods for changing free and upright citizens not only into grumbling slaves, but into serfs who in many respects accept their masters' values. They still think that they are following their own life goals and values, whereas in reality they have accepted the Nazis' values as their own.[19]

In accepting the Nazis' values as their own, prisoners embraced the definitions of reality and truth held by the Gestapo. Consequently, for a sociologist to undertake a study from the subordinate prisoners' "own standpoint" would be to conduct an investigation from the standpoint of the superordinate Gestapo. Furthermore, the absence of a unique perspective is not limited to such extreme situations as concentration camps. Gouldner makes a similar suggestion with respect to the perspective of Negroes vis-à-vis the dominant white culture in American society.[20] Erving Goffman, among others, has noted that patients in mental hospitals and inmates of corrective institutions adopt and consistently carry out the roles expected of them by their "superiors."[21] Once again, any study from the point of view of these subordinate groups would be ipso facto a study conducted from the point of view of superordinate groups.

In short, the conceptual confusion to which Becker has fallen prey is in assuming that to occupy a standpoint (that is, to be a member of some ranked group) one automatically possesses a unique perspective with its own value commitments. We have seen that this is not necessarily the case. The conclusion to be drawn is that even if it is true that all sociological research must be conducted from some point of view (a conclusion, it should be remembered, that is indefensible in so far as it presupposes the adequacy of the sociology of knowledge), it does not follow that such research is inevitably biased. In order to be biased the sociologist would have to accept uncritically the value commitments of a particular subordinate point of view to the exclusion of all other value commitments. This, of course, presupposes that the subordinate point of view has "its own" value commitments, an assumption that we have seen to be false in many instances. Therefore, it is not the case (contrary to Becker) that social scientific research is inevitably biased—even if we accept the dubious claim that it is always conducted from some standpoint.

The second example of conceptual confusion in Becker's analysis is his failure to clarify what it means "to *take* sides" or "to *adopt* a point of view" in such a way that bias is the inevitable result. As already noted, the general drift of Becker's argument is that in a society structured according to ranked groups and governed by the principle of a hierarchy of credibility, any social scientific study undertaken from the standpoint of a subordinate group is open to the charge of bias. To assume that subordinates have as much right to be heard as superordinates, to assume that they are as likely to tell the truth as they see it as superordinates, and to assume that their complaints should be investigated and given as much credence as the statements of responsible officials is to provoke the charge of bias. After all, the point of the hierarchy of credibility is that those at the top possess the right to define what is real and what is true. Consequently, Becker concludes that a social scientist who conducts his research from the standpoint of a subordinate group is "telling a story from their point of view," a situation inevitably characterized by bias.

This line of thought is particularly applicable to those disciplines of social science, such as the sociology of deviant behavior, that are interested in the study of subordinate groups. It may be less obvious, but according to Becker no less true, that "to tell a story" from *any* point of view is to be biased toward that perspective, even if the perspective is that of a superordinate group. Thus, a study of mental hospitals from the standpoint of doctors will be as biased as one from the standpoint of patients; a study of prisons from the standpoint of wardens will be as biased as one from the standpoint of inmates; and so on. Bias is ubiquitous for the social scientist because he must "tell his story" from someone's point of view.

Even if we permit to go unchallenged Becker's suggestion that the model of explanation in the social sciences is the construction of narratives, it is not the case that "telling a story" from some point of view entails a biased account. To see that this is so, we need only ask what the minimum requirements are for "telling a story" from a point of view. Three possibilities suggest themselves. I may be said to "tell a story" from the standpoint of X if: (1) I recount the same facts that X would recount if he were telling the story, even though my assessment of the facts may differ from X's assessment, or (2) my assessment of some situation in which X finds himself is the same as X's assessment even though I disagree with X about some of the facts pertaining to the case, or (3) I recount the same facts X would recount if he were telling the story and assess those facts in the same way X assesses them. If, for example, my wife has punished our older son for hitting his younger brother, I may be said to tell what happened from my older son's point of view if: (1) I describe in ever so vivid detail how the older son was painfully spanked even though I disagree that the punishment was unfair or (2) I acknowledge the unfairness of the punishment due to my younger son's taunts having brought about the altercation, even though I disagree that he was punished because my wife no longer loves him, or (3) I describe how he was painfully spanked and agree that the punishment was unfair.

In important respects the above example satisfies Becker's criteria for a situation in which biased reporting should be expected. A subordinate (a child) is in conflict with a superordinate (his mother). Assuming for the example that I tell the story from

the child's viewpoint, I either relate the events in the conflict as
he would relate them, or assess the conflict as he would assess it,
or relate and assess the conflict as he would be inclined to do.
Whichever of these three stances I take, my words imply that the
child has a right to be heard, that he is as likely as his mother to
tell the truth as he sees it, and that his complaints ought to be
given as much credence as the statements of his mother. Whichever stance I take, I am "telling the story" from his perspective.

The important question is: in viewing the conflict from the
child's perspective in any one of the three senses, have I become
his partisan spokesman? Clearly, in the first two instances I have
not. Even if I recount the facts of the conflict exactly as the child
would, I am not committed to his evaluation of those facts.
("Kicking your younger brother in the shins is not an appropriate
response to his mild taunts; thus, your punishment was just," I
might say.) Or, if the nature of the conflict is slightly different,
such that I agree with the complaint of unfair punishment in light
of the seriousness of the provocation, I am not committed to accept all of my son's beliefs about the facts of the case. ("No, your
mother still loves you; she was simply unaware of the provocation," I might observe.) It is only in the third instance—where I
accept my son's beliefs about the facts of the conflict and agree
with his assessment of those facts—that I am in danger of being
biased in his favor. I *need not* be biased even in this instance,
however, for the acceptance of my son's beliefs and evaluations
might come about only after I have weighed the beliefs and evaluations of others, in particular those of my younger son and of my
wife. No one, I suspect, other than the most extreme exponent of
the sociology of knowledge, will deny that at least sometimes I am
capable of understanding simultaneously the beliefs and evaluations of subordinates and superordinates, weighing the respective
merits of each, and coming to a decision about them. If I am capable of such a performance, there is no compelling reason to believe that I must be a partisan narrator whenever I "tell a story"
from someone's point of view.

My point is that in failing to clarify what he means by "taking sides" or "telling a story from some perspective," Becker mis-
takenly concludes that bias is inevitable in social scientific research. If, however, we keep in mind the distinction between

"accepting X's factual beliefs" and "accepting X's normative beliefs," the inevitability of bias is eliminated. [22] For, if the above analysis is correct, I can meaningfully be said "to tell a story from X's point of view" though I do not accept *all* his beliefs. Furthermore, since the indefensible character of the sociology of knowledge has already been noted, there is no compelling reason to think that I cannot accept *critically* all of X's beliefs. But so long as my acceptance is not mindless assent, bias is no longer an inevitable concomitant of "taking sides."

The second source of error, therefore, in Becker's account is his failure to clarify sufficiently the meaning of such key concepts as "points of view" and "telling a story from a point of view." In leaving these concepts vague Becker has overlooked two rather obvious points: that to occupy a social standpoint is not the same as to possess a unique perspective and that to "tell a story from some group's point of view" does not involve accepting uncritically *all* the beliefs and values of that group. Becker's failure to draw these distinctions lies at the basis of his mistaken belief that since all sociological research must be conducted from some point of view, it must inevitably be biased.

In conclusion, it should be noted that Professor Becker's view that there can be no objective (that is, value-free and unbiased) sociological research presupposes the truth of two propositions: (1) the sociologist must always conduct his investigations from some point of view and (2) all points of view are biased. I have argued that the first proposition can be accepted only if one accepts in turn the indefensible epistemology of the sociology of knowledge and that the second proposition is plausible only so long as the conceptual confusion that surrounds "adopting a point of view" and "taking sides" is left unresolved.

Since Becker gives no valid reasons to show these two propositions to be true, he has no valid reasons for stating that objective sociological research is intrinsically impossible. If (as I argue) Becker's analysis is applicable to all the social sciences (not just to sociology), it follows that he has given no valid reasons for thinking that value commitments and political sympathies inevitably enter into the conclusions of the social sciences.

"Whose side are we on?" may serve as a rallying cry for those social technicians who are members of what Noam Chomsky calls "the new mandarins.[23] It is not a fruitful starting point for reflection on problems in the philosophy of the social sciences.

NOTES

1. Howard S. Becker, "Whose Side Are We On?" *Social Problems*, 14 (Winter 1967), pp. 239-247. Alvin W. Gouldner, "The Sociologist as Partisan: Sociology and the Welfare State," *The American Sociologist*, 3 (May 1968), pp. 103-116. [Becker's essay is reprinted in its entirety in the present volume, pp. 107-121. The concluding sections of Gouldner's paper are also reprinted here, pp. 53-64. In the following notes, original page citations are followed by citations in parentheses of pages in this volume.]

2. See Gouldner's comments about the representative character of Becker's view of sociology, *ibid.*, p. 103.

3. Max Weber, *The Methodology of the Social Sciences* (New York: Free Press of Glencoe, 1949), p. 72.

4. Becker, *op. cit.*, p. 245 (116-117).

5. Gouldner, *op. cit.*, pp. 111-113.

6. Becker, *op. cit.*, p. 239 (107).

7. In emphasizing points of agreement between Becker and Gouldner, I do not want to suggest that there are no points of disagreement. Indeed, Gouldner (*op. cit.*, pp. 112-116), unlike Becker, thinks that the inevitable bias of sociological research is compatible with its objectivity. Whether or not Gouldner succeeds in making a case for this position is beside the point since the line of argument I shall develop is that neither Becker nor Gouldner provides convincing reasons for thinking that sociological research is inevitably biased. Since Becker and Gouldner are in agreement on this last point, the differences in their positions are less important than the similarities.

8. Becker, *op. cit.*, p. 245 (117).

9. *Ibid.*, p. 239 (108).

10. *Ibid.*, p. 241 (111).

11. *Ibid.*, p. 243 (114).

12. See Becker's reference to George H. Mead, *ibid.*, p. 245 (116-117).

13. Karl Mannheim, *Ideology and Utopia,* translated by Louis Wirth and Edward Shils (London: Routledge and Kegan Paul, 1954), pp. 243, 259.

14. Gouldner, *op. cit.,* p. 103.

15. A possible gambit for someone wishing to counter my criticism of the sociology of knowledge would be to rely upon Bertrand Russell's "theory of logical types" as a means to vitiate the charge of self-referential inconsistency. Although the matter cannot be discussed here in detail, I do not believe such a defense can succeed. In the first place, one way in which paradoxes can be resolved according to the theory of types is by treating as meaningless all propositions that are concerned with attributes or classes in general. Since the sociology of knowledge is a theory about the *general* class of knowledge claims, it would have to be declared meaningless under the theory of types. In the second place, the theory of types has problems of its own. If it applies, as it must, to all classes of propositions, it cannot even be stated without violating its own principle. For a detailed discussion of this last point, see Paul Weiss, "The Theory of Types," *Mind,* n.s. 37 (July 1928), pp. 338-348, and F. B. Fitch, "Self-Reference in Philosophy," *Mind,* n.s. 55 (January 1946), pp. 64-73.

16. Becker, *op. cit.,* p. 240 (109).

17. I do not consider my critique of the sociology of knowledge to be a refutation of Mannheim's, or any other representative's, *total* position. After all, in the case of Mannheim (if I understand him correctly) something very close to the position I defend is held open to the "free intelligentsia" who are capable of gaining "relational objectivity." My criticism is limited to that *part* of the sociology of knowledge that stresses the social and/or cultural relativity of *all* knowledge claims. This is the thesis Becker's conclusions presuppose, and it is relativism of this sort that is common to, and at the base of, both the sociology of knowledge and older forms of historicism.

18. Ludwig Wittgenstein, *Philosophical Investigations,* translated by G. E. M. Anscombe (Oxford: Basil Blackwell, 1958), II, p. xiv.

19. Bruno Bettelheim, "Individual and Mass Behavior in Extreme Situations," *Journal of Abnormal and Social Psychology,* 38 (October 1943), p. 451.

20. Gouldner, *op. cit.,* p. 107.

21. Cf. Erving Goffman, *Asylums: Essays on the Social Situation of Mental Patients and Other Inmates* (Garden City, N.Y.: Doubleday Anchor, 1961).

22. In distinguishing between "factual beliefs" and "normative beliefs" I am not adopting a position that assigns "facts" and "values" to logically separate categories, as did logical positivism during the 1930s. Subsequent studies in ethics (among other subjects) have shown this categorization to be too simplistic. The point I wish to make in employing the above distinction is to isolate the different areas of agreement and disagreement that are open to anyone called upon to assess the beliefs of others. The example I have constructed should make clear this limited use of the distinction.

23. Cf. Noam Chomsky, "The Menace of Liberal Scholarship," *The New York Review of Books,* 11 (January 2, 1969), pp. 29-38.

9

Reply to Riley's
"Partisanship and Objectivity"

Howard S. Becker

Riley may have a quarrel, but it isn't with me. Evidently I failed to make the argument of my paper sufficiently unambiguous to prevent the misinterpretation of my position he has made. In fact, I pretty much agree with what he has to say and will only suggest how he might have arrived at that interpretation and then restate what I think in such a fashion that he will see our essential agreement. Those who hold the position he attributes to me and wish to defend it will have to do so for themselves.

We can speak of bias in social science research in at least these two ways:

1. Work is biased when it presents statements of fact that are demonstrably incorrect, the demonstration being according to accepted scientific canons of evidence, and when those incorrect empirical statements consistently arise from the researcher's opinions, prejudices, values, emotions, or whatever. I believe Riley has this meaning in mind in criticizing my paper. It is the meaning of bias that most frequently concerns scientists.

2. Laymen, the subjects of research, politically interested parties, and others speak of bias in a quite different sense. They call social science research biased when its results favor or appear to

Reprinted by permission from *The American Sociologist*, 6 (February 1971), p. 13. Copyright © 1971 by The American Sociological Association.

favor one side or another in a controversy. Thus, politicians accuse the research sponsored by the Presidential Commission on
Obscenity and Pornography of being biased because its results
favor, from any viewpoint concerned with the relative costs and
benefits of public policy, a libertarian approach to pornography.
Conclusions that disagree with prejudices must be wrong—when
politicians do not accuse scientists of dishonesty, they accuse
them of bias.

Work that is quite unbiased in the first sense may be open to
charges of bias in the second sense. It should be clear that I concerned myself almost entirely with bias in the second sense. My
argument, in brief, was that we cannot avoid being subjected to
the charge of bias in that second sense. The organizations and
communities we study and the people in them who hold positions
high enough to be held responsible for their operation promote
myths about themselves: about how peaceful they are, about how
well they perform the services and functions they purport to perform, and so on. The most objective and apolitical research imag-
inable, if it shows that these myths are factually incorrect, will
probably be accused of bias by those who see the results as criticism or exposé of their stewardship. If it does not dispute these
myths, those who occupy subordinate positions in those same organizations and communities may complain that the research is
biased in the opposite direction. Since the people holding superordinate positions in organizations and communities are more
likely to promulgate and profit from fallacious myths, they are
likewise more likely to complain that research is biased, though
this is not inevitably the case. These circumstances account for
the frequent suggestion that sociological research favors the interests of subordinates. In situations where the organization or community is not stratified, or where the strata do not consciously
have different interests, the above analysis will not apply. I think
such situations rare in contemporary societies.

Saying that our research, insofar as it deals with matters of
public concern, will inevitably confirm or impugn conventional
wisdom on those matters in no way suggests or implies that objective research is not possible. Riley ought not to be so surprised
at my failure to accept the tenets of such a totally relativistic epistemology as he describes. My argument doesn't presuppose those

tenets, because I distinguish the two meanings of bias Riley runs together and treats as one. We don't fully succeed in achieving objectivity in the first sense I described, but it isn't, in principle, an unattainable goal and is, in my view, worth striving for. I do so all the time. Objectivity in the second sense does seem to me in principle unattainable, although if Riley makes a persuasive argument on this point I'm willing to listen to reason, not being any more of a nut than absolutely necessary these days. (I might point out that the quotation Riley finds so important, "there is no position from which sociological research can be done that is not biased in one or another way," occurs late in the essay, by which time I thought it clear that I was speaking of bias in the second of the senses referred to above.)

Given my position on the possibility of objective research, I hope Riley will now see the logical status of the various propositions I make about social structure. I hope he will no longer find them paradoxical, but will see that they are what we might call speculative generalizations, propositions capable of being tested by data gathered in the ways we now have available to us. I hope he sees that what I said does not necessarily entail accepting the view that "the sociologist can neither know nor use data which do not lend support to the value commitments of 'his side.' " I hope he will see a fourth possible interpretation of "telling a story" from the standpoint of X, the one I actually meant: the sociologist tells the story from the standpoint of X when his theoretically informed and objectively assessed conclusions about the relations of X and Y cast doubt on the way Y describes those relations and lends some credence to the way X describes them. I leave the application of this definition to the example of the spanking of Riley's elder son as an exercise for the reader.

10

Comments
on Howard Becker's "Reply"

Gresham Riley

In his reply to my paper "Partisanship and Objectivity in the Social Sciences," Professor Becker contends that his position does not imply that objective research in the social sciences is impossible and that he is not committed to the tenets of the relativistic epistemology I ascribed to him.

Becker's self-defense rests on two senses of bias that he distinguishes as follows: (1) research is biased when it presents statements of fact that are demonstrably false according to accepted scientific canons of evidence and when such statements arise from the researcher's "opinions, prejudices, values, emotions, or whatever" and (2) research is *open to the charge of bias* when "its results favor or appear to favor one side or another in a controversy." Armed with this distinction, Becker argues that the two senses of bias are logically independent; that he concerned himself in "Whose Side Are We On?" "almost entirely" with bias in the second sense; and that I was able to charge him with methodological subjectivism and epistemological relativism only by running together and treating as one the two different senses.

I wish to make several points about Becker's two senses of bias, because it seems to me that they reinforce my original criticisms rather than provide an avenue of escape from them.

First, note that Becker has not distinguished two *meanings* of bias. Although the first sense is one possible meaning, the second sense is less a definition than a specification of the context within which research might be *accused* of bias. At times, Becker himself seems to be aware that merely to favor one side or another in a controversy is not the same as to be biased, for in "Whose Side Are We On?" he separates two issues: (a) accusations of bias on the ground that sides have been taken and (b) the justification of such accusations.[1] In other words, what it means to *be* biased cannot be equated with the taking of sides, even though the taking of sides may lead to the *accusation* of bias. Bias, then, is not constituted merely by favoring one side or another in a controversy; everything depends on the conduct of the inquiry, on the way in which one has arrived at such a position. This, however, is just another way of stating a major conclusion of my paper—namely, to occupy a standpoint is not necessarily to be a *partisan* spokesman for that standpoint.

Second, I am baffled by Becker's claim that his original argument was that "we cannot avoid being subjected to the charge of bias in [the] second sense." Since, as we have seen, the second sense is not a definition of bias at all, I can only understand Becker's reformulated position to be: It is inevitable that social scientists will be *accused* of bias, rather than it is inevitable that social scientists will *be* biased. In clarifying his position, therefore, Becker has changed it, for in his original essay he states clearly that sociological research cannot avoid *being* biased in one or another way.[2] The original view at least had the virtue of being interesting even if (for the reasons I advanced) it was indefensible. The new position is hardly interesting because, given the nature of social controversy, it is probably trivially true.

Finally, although Becker's second "sense" of bias is not a definition at all, it does focus attention on a major concern of his essay. As previously indicated, Becker separates the issues of (a) accusations of bias and (b) whether or not a given accusation of bias is justified. In my paper I did not stress this separation of issues and consequently did not dwell on Becker's extended discussion of the circumstances in which a sociologist is likely to be accused of bias. This neglect, I believe, is the reason Becker accuses me of misinterpreting his position as being committed to methodological subjectivism and epistemological relativism. The question therefore becomes: If Becker's original concern with the circumstances that lead to the accusation of bias is acknowledged, do my criticisms of his position lose their point? I think not.

The greater part of Becker's essay was devoted to (a) above. His distinction between apolitical and political cases of controversy was made in that context, and this distinction led in turn to a lengthy exploration of "by whom, in what situations and for what reasons sociologists will be accused of bias and distortion." The details of this exploration are less important than the fact that, having concluded it, Becker turned in the final pages of his essay to the question of the *truth* of the accusations—that is, to (b) above. What he said in regard to this question is important.

Becker began with what he called a "partial answer"— namely, "there is no position from which sociological research can be done that is not biased in one or another way."[3] Note, however, that this partial answer is *irrelevant* to the question of the truth of accusations of bias unless one assumes that it is not possible for sociologists to avoid taking sides and that to take sides is inevitably to be biased in favor of that point of view. Becker does in fact make these assumptions, and it is for these reasons (among others, as I argued) that he is committed to the subjectivism and relativism in question. Furthermore, in expanding his "partial answer" Becker denied sociologists access to possible safeguards against the bias that inevitably results from taking sides. In particular, he did so with respect to the use of sociological methodology ("the tools and techniques of our discipline"), to the attempt to see everyone in a ranked social structure as (in a sense) a subordinate, and to the attempt to limit the scope of sociological conclusions.[4] In short, when we put together what Becker says about the truth of accusations of bias, his answer is that such accusations are *always* true since bias (and here a meaning other than Becker's "second sense" is required) is unavoidable. Once again, this is a conclusion that presupposes the theoretical commitments I ascribed to Becker.

It seems that in separating the two issues above and in concentrating on the former, Becker thinks that in his essay he was raising straightforward empirical questions and answering them on empirical rather than theoretical grounds. In particular, he thinks that his answers were not based on theoretical assumptions of a subjective or relativistic sort. Becker is mistaken (I believe) in this assumption, and his mistake is concealed from him by the further belief that his concern all along was "almost entirely with bias in the second sense."

To see that Becker is mistaken, all one need do is to raise once again the questions by whom, in what circumstances, and for what reasons sociologists will be accused of bias and to give the answers which Becker (in light of his position as I have sketched it) ought to have given. By whom? Why, by everyone, including the sociologist himself. In what circumstances? Why, in all circumstances, including the adoption of the superordinate's point of view in apolitical controversies.[5] For what reasons? Why, because of the inevitability of bias. But why (and this is the most important question) is bias inevitable? Because, according to Becker:

1. To have values or not to have values....This dilemma, which seems so painful to so many, actually does not exist, for one of its horns is imaginary. For it to exist, one would have to assume, as some apparently do, that it is indeed possible to do research that is uncontaminated by personal and political sympathies. I propose to argue that it is not possible and, therefore, that the question is not whether we should take sides, since we inevitably will, but rather whose side are we on.

2. In the greatest variety of subject areas and in work done by all different methods at our disposal, we cannot avoid taking sides, for reasons firmly based in social structure.

3. ...there is no position from which sociological research can be done that is not biased in one or another way. [For] we must always look at the matter from someone's point of view.[6]

These passages (the first two of which do not occur "late in the essay" but rather in the opening three paragraphs) make clear that it is in appearance only that Becker sought empirical answers to empirical questions. In fact, the questions were resolved in advance on theoretical grounds that do commit Becker (in the way I originally argued) to the subjectivistic methodology and the relativistic epistemology which he is so loath to accept. It appears that the basis for a quarrel with Becker still exists.

NOTES

1. Howard S. Becker, "Whose Side Are We On?" *Social Problems,* 14 (Winter 1967), p. 240 (109).

2. *Ibid.,* p. 245 (116).

3. *Ibid.*

4. *Ibid.,* pp. 246-247 (118-120).

5. Cf. *ibid.,* pp. 242, 243 (112, 114).

6. *Ibid.,* pp. 239, 245 (107-108, 116).

Selected Bibliography

Essays reprinted in this collection are not included in this list.

Becker, Howard P. *Through Values to Social Interpretation.* Westport, Conn.: Greenwood Press, 1968.

Bendix, Reinhard. *Social Science and the Distrust of Reason.* Berkeley: University of California Press, 1951.

Bisbee, Eleanor. "Objectivity in the Social Sciences," *Philosophy of Science,* 4 (1937), pp. 371-382.

Bottomore, T. B. "Some Reflections on the Sociology of Knowledge," *British Journal of Sociology,* 7 (1956), pp. 52-58.

Bramson, Leon. *The Political Context of Sociology.* Princeton: University Press, 1961, Chapters 1 and 7.

Braybrooke, David. "The Relevance of Norms to Political Description," *American Political Science Review,* 52 (1958), pp. 989-1006.

Child, Arthur. "The Problem of Truth in the Sociology of Knowledge," *Ethics,* 58 (1947), pp. 18-34.

Dahrendorf, Ralf. "Values and Social Science: The Value Dispute in Perspective" in *Essays in the Theory of Society.* Stanford, Cal.: Stanford University Press, 1968.

Diesing, P. "Objectivism vs. Subjectivism in the Social Sciences," *Philosophy of Science*, 33 (June 1966), pp. 124-133.

Easton, David. "The New Revolution in Political Science," *American Political Science Review*, 63 (December 1969), pp. 1051-1061.

Eister, Allan W. "Values, Sociology and the Sociologists," *Sociological Analysis*, 25 (Summer 1964), pp. 108-112.

Eulau, Heinz. "Values and Behavioral Science: Neutrality Revisited," *Antioch Review*, 28 (Summer 1968), pp. 160-167.

Furfey, Paul Hanly. "Sociological Science and the Problem of Values," in L. Gross (ed.), *Symposium on Sociological Theory*. New York: Harper and Row, 1959, pp. 509-530.

Gewirth, Alan. "Subjectivism and Objectivism in the Social Sciences," *Philosophy of Science*, 21 (April 1954), pp. 157-163.

Gibson, Quentin. *The Logic of Social Enquiry*. London: Routledge and Kegan Paul, 1960, Chapters 6 and 7.

Gillispie, C. C. *The Edge of Objectivity*. Princeton: Princeton University Press, 1960.

Gluck, S. E. "The Epistemology of Mannheim's Sociology of Knowledge," *Methodos*, 6 (1954), pp. 225-234.

Golightly, C. L. "Value as a Scientific Concept," *Journal of Philosophy*, 53 (March 29, 1956), pp. 233-245.

Gouldner, Alvin W. "Anti-Minotaur: The Myth of a Value-Free Sociology," *Social Problems*, 9 (Winter 1962), pp. 199-213.

Gouldner, Alvin W. "The Sociologist as Partisan: Sociology and the Welfare State," *The American Sociologist*, 3 (May 1968), pp. 103-116.

Gray, David J. "Value-Free Sociology: A Doctrine of Hypocrisy and Irresponsibility," *Sociological Quarterly*, 9 (Spring 1968), pp. 176-185.

Gunther, M., and K. Reshaur. "Science and Values in Political 'Science'," *Philosophy of the Social Sciences*, 1 (May 1971), pp. 113-121.

Hartung, F. E. "Problems of the Sociology of Knowledge," *Philosophy of Science*, 19 (1952), pp. 17-32.

Heelan, Patrick A. "Scientific Objectivity and Framework Trans-positions," *Philosophical Studies,* 19 (1970), pp. 55-70.

Hinshaw, V. G., Jr. "Epistemological Relativism and the Sociology of Knowledge," *Philosophy of Science,* 15 (1948), pp. 4-10.

Horowitz, Irving Louis. "Social Science Objectivity and Value Neutrality: Historical Problems and Projections," *Diogenes,* 39 (1962), pp. 17-44.

Jeffrey, R. F. "Valuation and Acceptance of Scientific Hypotheses," *Philosophy of Science,* 23 (July 1956), pp. 237-246.

Kaufman, Arnold S. "The Aims of Scientific Activity," *The Monist,* 52 (July 1968), pp. 374-389.

Klappholz, Kurt. "Value Judgments and Economics," *British Journal for the Philosophy of Science,* 15 (1964), pp. 97-114.

Koehler, Wolfgang. *The Place of Value in a World of Fact.* New York: Liveright, 1938.

Kuhn, Thomas S. *The Structure of Scientific Revolutions.* Chicago: University of Chicago Press, 1970.

Kuklick, Bruce. "The Mind of the Historian," *History and Theory,* 8 (1969), pp. 313-331.

Lawson, Robert M. "On the Possibility of an Objective Social Science," *Kinesis,* 2 (Fall 1969), pp. 3-14.

Leach, James. "Explanation and Value Neutrality," *British Journal for the Philosophy of Science,* 19 (1968), pp. 93-108.

Leach, James. "Historical Objectivity and Value Neutrality," *Inquiry,* 11 (Winter 1968), pp. 349-367.

Levi, I. "Must the Scientist Make Value Judgments?" *Journal of Philosophy,* 58 (May 26, 1960), pp. 345-357.

Lynd, Robert S. *Knowledge for What?* Princeton: Princeton University Press, 1940.

Machlup, Fritz. "Are the Social Sciences Really Inferior?" in Maurice Natanson (ed.), *Philosophy of the Social Sciences: A Reader.* New York: Random House, 1963, pp. 158-180.

Mackenzie, P. T. "Fact and Value," *Mind,* 76 (April 1967), pp. 228-237.

Mandelbaum, Maurice. *The Problem of Historical Knowledge: An Answer to Relativism.* New York: Liveright, 1938.

Mannheim, Karl. *Ideology and Utopia.* New York: Harcourt, Brace and World, 1936, Chapter 5.

Martin, Michael. "Referential Variance and Scientific Objectivity," *British Journal for the Philosophy of Science,* 22 (February 1971), pp. 17-26.

McLaughlin, Andrew. "Science, Reason and Value," *Theory and Decision,* 1 (December 1970), pp. 121-137.

Meehan, Eugene J. *Value Judgment and Social Science.* Homewood, Ill.: Dorsey Press, 1969.

Myrdal, Gunnar. "Methodological Note on Facts and Valuations in Social Science," in *An American Dilemma.* New York: Harper and Row, 1944, pp. 1035-1064.

Myrdal, Gunnar. *Objectivity in Social Research.* New York: Pantheon Books, 1969.

Nagel, Ernest. *The Structure of Science.* New York: Harcourt, Brace and World, 1961, Chapter 13.

Parsons, Talcott. "Evaluation and Objectivity in Social Science: An Interpretation of Max Weber's Contribution" in *Sociological Theory and Modern Society.* New York: Free Press, 1967, pp. 79-101.

Passmore, J. A. "Can the Social Sciences Be Value-Free?" in Herbert Feigl and May Brodbeck (eds.), *Readings in the Philosophy of Science.* New York: Appleton-Century-Crofts, 1953, pp. 674-676.

Piccone, Paul. "Functionalism, Teleology, and Objectivity," *The Monist,* 52 (July 1968), pp. 408-423.

Rescher, Nicholas. "Values and the Explanation of Behaviour," *The Philosophical Quarterly,* 17 (April 1967), pp. 130-136.

Roshwald, M. "Value-Judgments in the Social Sciences," *British Journal for the Philosophy of Science,* 6 (1955), pp. 186-208.

Rossi, Pietro. "Scientific Objectivity and Value Hypotheses," *International Social Science Journal,* 17 (1965), pp. 64-70.

Rudner, Richard S. "The Scientist *qua* Scientist Makes Value Judgments," *Philosophy of Science,* 20 (January 1953), pp. 1-6.

Ryan, Alan. *The Philosophy of the Social Sciences.* New York: Pantheon Books, 1970, Chapter 10.

Schaff, Adam. "On Objective Truth in Sociology," *Soviet Studies in Philosophy,* 6 (Fall 1967), pp. 33-38.

Scheffler, Israel. *Science and Subjectivity.* New York: Bobbs-Merrill, 1967.

"Some Radical Perspectives in Sociology," *Sociological Inquiry,* 40 (Winter 1970).

Sposito, Garrison. "Does a Generalized Heisenberg Principle Operate in the Social Sciences?" *Inquiry,* 12 (Fall 1969), pp. 356-361.

Stack, George J. "Facts and Values in Science," *Journal of Thought,* 4 (April 1969), pp. 125-139.

Stack, George J. "Value and Fact," *Journal of Value Inquiry,* 3 (Fall 1969), pp. 205-216.

Strauss, Leo. "Natural Right and the Distinction Between Facts and Values," in Maurice Natanson (ed.), *Philosophy of the Social Sciences: A Reader.* New York: Random House, 1963, pp. 419-457.

Weber, Max. *The Methodology of the Social Sciences.* Translated and edited by Edward A. Shils and Henry A. Finch. New York: Free Press of Glencoe, 1949.

Winch, Peter. *The Idea of a Social Science and Its Relation to Philosophy.* New York: Humanities Press, 1967.

Wolfe, Alan, and Marvin Surkin (eds.). *An End to Political Science: The Caucus Papers.* New York: Basic Books, 1970.

Wolin, Sheldon S. "Political Science as a Vocation," *American Political Science Review,* 63 (December 1969), pp. 1062-1082.

17-401

DATE DUE

JUL 8 1975			
JUL 8 1976 PL			
30 505 JOSTEN'S			